Star Spangled Banter ©

Star Spangled Banter [©]

By

Doug Hecox

ISBN: 1-58721-176-9

1st Books-rev. 7/26/00

About the Book

Frustrated about America? Surrounded by idiots? Afraid of the dark? Doug Hecox gives voice to your concerns and more in "Star Spangled Banter," a collection of essays on everything from driver-side airbags to campaign finance reform to the evil of clipping your fingernails in public.

Part Hunter Thompson, part Homer Simpson and part Dennis Miller, "Star Spangled Banter" reflects the skewed view of one of America's next great satirists. Readers will immediately see that Doug's perspective is unique – and hysterical. Suggesting that cremation is an unhealthy form of littering, that responsible parents will remove their children's teeth and replace them with dentures, or that "Who's Who"-style books are the first place aliens look when they abduct humans for their intergalactic space zoos, Doug runs the gamut as he examines modern society.

If you like the Onion, National Lampoon or Mad Magazine, you'll love "Star Spangled Banter." Because this book is not yet available on audiotape, you'll have to read "Star Spangled Banter" aloud while you drive. Make sure to buy extra copies – one for your car, one for the ambulance crew and one for the others at the scene of the accident. If laughter is the best medicine, you'll be glad you did!

Dedicated to….

My parents, Dick and Connie, who gave me love;
My brother, Andy, who gave me resolve;
and Laura, who told me I wasn't crazy and kept a
straight face

Table of Contents

Preface

Hopefully what follows is proof that, though increasingly reserved for late night television monologues, satire and political humor continue to have a place in newspapers and on bookshelves. And in hotel nightstands, if only the Gideons hadn't forwarded their calls to the Rosicrucians.

Readers of my weekly column, "Doug, Writer of Wrongs," which originated in the Daily Times of Rawlins, Wyoming, have been aware of my takes on topical news events and general social commentary since March 1997. Some of "Star Spangled Banter" is material that was featured previously in newspapers but wasn't worded quite right to suit me. That said, my steadfast fans will appreciate that much of the book is brand-spanking new.

Be you new reader or longtime fan, I've taken the time to make sure "Star Spangled Banter" is just right, so I hope you enjoy it. If you're reading this for news content, you may be pleased to know that the quotations and factual information used herein were culled from both the Washington Post *AND* the legitimate press.

If one is reading this just for the jokes, one is missing out on some of the fun. Good satire, I'm told, is humor that makes a point. This is not to insinuate or trivialize the pointed humor of farce, lampoon or parody (as exemplified in The Onion, National Lampoon and Mad Magazine) or even the simple day-to-day buffoonery made popular by Congress. Simply put, one is hard pressed to make the distinction between the definitions of the varied forms of humor. Though it isn't easy, one knows it when one sees it -- sort of like spotting a prostitute at a cosmetics convention.

Writing a book is not easy but, without question, the most difficult part is in coming up with a suitable title. It's tougher now than ever before to name a book, as all the good titles have been taken. The "Bible," the "Encyclopedia Brittanica" and even "Roget's Thesaurus" all are great names, which probably explains their commercial success. Before settling on "Star Spangled Banter," I gave a lot of thought to the following possibilities:

The Uncommon Denominator
Pith and Vinegar, While-U-Wait
Halfwit, Will Travel
Doug's High-Fiber Book of Psycho Babble
It's Hard to Soar With the Eagles (When You're a Dumbass)[1]
Al Franken Is Also A Big Fat Idiot[2]
The Self-Fulfilling Prophet
Jung At Heart and A Freud of Nothing
Flies Don't Like Bird Doo (and Other Observations)
Doug's Previously Untitled Book of Fun
No Good Can Come Of This
Bedtime Stories For the Criminally Inane
My Scrubbing Bubbles Refuse to Talk
Home, Home on Deranged
The Bible II[3]
or (my personal favorite) --
10 Buy This Book
20 Goto 10[4]

In "Star Spangled Banter," I hope readers will come away with a few laughs, if not an appreciation for America and her system of government. However, readers offended by any part of this book should simply return unused portion with proof of purchase and prepare to be featured in my next book, tentatively entitled "People Who Need A Sense of Humor Worse Than A Refund."

---

[1] I figure the cover art could be a donkey in a dunce cap.

[2] A backhanded reference to Franken's dismal tome "Rush Limbaugh Is a Big Fat Idiot."

[3] It would be a sequel to that OTHER book -- the one that's been topping the charts for the last 103,000 weeks.

[4] This was ruled out as being too "BASIC" for the average, non-computer programmer.

Good Ideas, Told Sensibly

*"There is no possibility of being witty without a little ill-nature;
the malice of a good thing is the barb that makes it stick."*

-- Richard Brinsley Sheridan, British Dramatist

April Fool's Day Prank Amnesty Sought

Some speculate that the casual nature of television violence contributes to increased social callousness. Thanks to television shows like "The Bugs Bunny and Tweety Show" and "The Simpsons," Americans think nothing of dropping huge boulders on co-workers, nor in offering friends dynamite shaped like cigars. In certain social circles, it is considered impolite NOT to.

If true, social norms -- or the "limits" imposed on certain activities -- of one generation are ignored by their successors. For example, many children today feel their school supplies should include a handgun. Four decades ago, all students needed for protection was a switchblade knife and pomade. A generation before, a porkpie hat, a raccoon coat and a potato masher from the Great War was all the protection an American needed. Alas, those days are gone. It takes a great deal more than a potato masher to survive in today's modern world because Americans are more callous than ever before.

How desensitized are we? In the good old days, Americans frequently would stop to help stranded motorists on the highway. Now we don't even slow down unless there is blood and broken glass. This is why, to ensure that others will stop to help me if I need it, I always carry blood and broken windshield glass with me. It's cheaper than AAA, and more effective than the "bared" leg routine of days gone by. This may explain why the Surface Transportation Policy Project reported in 1999 that aggressive driving-related deaths are on the rise. Apparently, folks *not* carrying blood and broken windshields are choosing to improvise.

However, with our callous nation approaching the most dangerous holiday of them all – April Fool's Day – special precautions must be taken. At issue is whether legislators should pass laws to protect the public from increasingly "over the top" April Fool's Day pranks. To wit: three pie-throwers in California, calling themselves the Biotic Baking Brigade, were convicted January 19, 1999, of battery for throwing cherry, pumpkin and tofu

3

pies at San Francisco Mayor Willie Brown during a speech the previous November. Though the pie-throwing trio each received six-month jail terms, they escaped a charge of "assault on a public official" which carries stiffer punishment.

Unfortunately, most – if not all – city councils, state legislatures and even Congress, deny the need for April Fool's Day protection efforts. In talking with many mayors across the country, I was told consistently "We are not planning to enact any such ordinances," "There is little evidence to support such actions," and "Stop calling me."

April Fool's Day 1998 opened my eyes to the need for such ordinances. As a comedian, it is my professional duty to make fun where I can. Thus, it was my April Foolish responsibility to replace the driver-side airbag in my ex-girlfriend's car with a "whoopie cushion."

For those who don't know, the whoopie cushion – the crowdpleasing low-note legacy of vaudeville – is much more popular in dining rooms and nursing home wheelchairs. I thought my girlfriend would find it funny but boy was MY face red! Not as red as hers, mind you, due to an unfortunate combination of too little makeup and too much pavement. She doesn't call me anymore, so my heart is nearly as broken as her windshield.

Believing that every cloud has a silver lining, as frequently as her intermittent consciousness would allow, I would point out that her iron-lung machine has more legroom than her Festiva did. Unfortunately, remarks like that did about as much to lighten her mood as my well-intended "Singing Kevorkiangram." She was in and out of a coma for weeks. It didn't really change our sex life, of course, except her parents were the ones screaming "Oh God!" Her eyes said "Yes," but her doctors said "No."

"Her iron-lung machine has more legroom than her Festiva did."

The previous April Fool's Day saw me switching a blind man's Visine with Wite-Out. He never noticed, of course, but his eyes now make him look like a zombie. Thank goodness for sunglasses.

Protect yourself this April from America's increasingly careless sense of humor. Please contact your local, state and Federal officials and find out where they stand on the issue of April Fool's Day protection. We owe it to our families and neighborhoods to take a stand against April Fool's Day hi-jinks. Time is of the essence. The pie-throwers, exploding cigars and driver-side whoopie cushions may be closer than you think.

Olympics Give Me the Red, White and Blues

*T*he world is a patchwork of guilty pleasures. Cuba has cigars, Russia has caviar and America has the demolition derby. Situated at the end of the week-long county fair, the derby is the dessert to a satisfying meal of rodeos, stock shows, arts, crafts and even a parade. Fans never tire of the derby's symphony of tearing metal and hissing radiator hoses.

The demolition derby is perhaps the most popular, yet unsung, extreme sport America has produced. Why it isn't an Olympic sport remains a mystery, though there is hope it will be someday. Attendance at the wildly-popular event suggests there is nothing more satisfying than watching cars collide. As I see it, the ideal derby car is a rental. An equally good choice is the Vatican's "Popemobile." After all, crashing into the Pope is sure to earn at least one black flag, if not outright disqualification or eternal damnation.

However, a popular choice for those who don't buy their cars at Holy See Auto Motors are late-1960s model Chrysler Newports. As any derby buff will tell you, the Newport is to cars as aircraft carriers are to rowboats. Drivers often look like they're wearing a helmet inside a mobile home with the doors welded shut. The car is so big, the back seat is actually a three-piece living room set.

As the world prepares for the Olympics, many suggest the games are rife with foreign events that put Americans at a competitive disadvantage. Did George Washington ever use tae kwan do as a lad? Did Abraham Lincoln ever speedskate around an ice rink like Hans Christian Andersen? It's only a matter of time until running with the bulls, jai alai, firewalking and yodeling are introduced, and American teams are hastily assembled in Colorado Springs.

More importantly, there are many events that seem less athletic than artistic. Ice dancing, for example. What the hell is that? If ice dancing can earn someone a gold medal, rollerskating should too.

Take away the ice and all you've got is "couples' skate" at any smalltown roller rink.

> "If ice dancing can earn someone a gold medal, rollerskating should too."

Clearly, our only hope lies in a pre-emptive Olympic strike. Americans should band together to promote the inclusion of rodeo events. If one can win a gold medal in curling -- the ridiculous sport known to millions as "extreme shuffleboard" -- it stands to reason that events requiring real athletic ability should be included. America's proud heritage of ranching offers many activities worthy of consideration.

To their credit, the Olympics currently use horses in equestrian events. Because it involves elements of gymnastics, sprinting, weightlifting and wrestling, calf roping should be an Olympic event, too. My uncle Jake would be a worthy contender. As a rancher, he practices roping every day because his business depends on it. Once, when experimenting with performance-enhancing steroids, he roped the trailer hitch of a passing pickup -- which he then wrestled to the ground. In record time, I might add. It made the driver unhappy, not to mention the rest of the funeral procession, so he vowed to never use steroids again.

Fencing is currently an Olympic event. Unfortunately, it doesn't involve wire, fenceposts or much of anything related to the fencing that ranchers are familiar with. The upper muckity-mucks in the Olympics should either rename the sport, or change fencing to include post-hole digging and barbed wire stretching.

Bull riding is another natural for the Olympics. Jake disagrees and, instead, thinks that bull shooting should be an event. This is because he could win a gold-medal in shooting the bull -- and he knows it. Similarly, my cousin Dee could get a gold medal in corn-on-the-cob eating if it were an event. Of course, Dee's overbite gives her a competitive edge.

Like many farmers, my grandfather enjoys driving his tractor down the road. It isn't very fast, but he loves seeing how many city drivers he can make wish that he'd turn off the road to let them by.

8

They honk, they fume, they try to pass in the other lane -- only to find another tractor heading toward them. What a rush! The gold medallist in the Olympic "traffic-blocking" event could be decided by whoever gets the most folks piled up behind them in the space of five miles.

A perennial winter event, also worthy of the Olympics, is coyote sniping. This may not be as sportsmanlike as some would like -- but it'd sure make good use of an activity ranchers are going to do anyway. If coyotes know what's good for them, they won't skulk around the herd of anyone gunning for a gold medal in shooting coyotes.

The Winter Olympics should definitely include the chopping of holes in ice-covered stock tanks and in frozen creeks so the herd can get a drink. I tip my hat to the rancher who taught his critters to eat snow. If nothing else, it seems like an easy way to make "ice milk." Most cows wouldn't have come up with an idea like that and would die of dehydration before realizing that snow IS water. This is why the winters of ranchers are a series of frequent hikes through knee-deep drifts and dozens of thirsty cows.

These are just a few thoughts from a well-meaning American fed up with the increasingly foreign nature of the Olympics. Hopefully, officials will include a few red, white and blue events in upcoming games. Speaking of which, I better gas up my Newport and start practicing for the traffic-blocking event. They don't just give those gold medals away.

Give Shoeless Passengers the Boot

*A*s a comedian, I not only have to be funny at all times but I also have to travel quite a bit. Given a choice, I prefer flying to driving or riding the train because I enjoy airports. Bigger airports, that is. Small airports have small runways. One hasn't lived until one has landed on a grass strip in the middle of Nebraska. The pilot informed us that, because so few planes land there, the runway also serves as a golf course during the summer. She then suggested we hunch down in our seats to avoid being hit by a hail of mulligans from novices at the driving range.

Small planes are always an adventure. Smaller airlines are, too. On longer flights, mainstream airlines often treat the passengers to an in-flight movie and a snack. I don't want to name the airline I was on but it was one of those cheap ones. How cheap, you may ask? The snack was an apple passed around to everyone, and it wasn't very filling because of the one-bite limit.

For the in-flight entertainment, there was no movie either. All they had was the *script* of a movie which passengers were invited to act out. As one might imagine, it was a little weird doing scenes from "Alive" at 30,000 feet. The vegetarian passengers were quick to complain, so we skipped ahead a few pages and ate them. Say what you want about vegetarians but you can definitely taste a difference.

Later, a flight attendant announced we were going to play in-flight Trivial Pursuit and the winner would get to disembark first. Unfortunately, the questions were all about how to operate the oxygen mask in the event of an emergency and how to turn your seat cushion into a flotation device. No one did very well. However, it did give me the opportunity to consider that, if there ever was an "unscheduled water landing," the last thing I want strapped close to my face is the foam cushion a billion other people sat on while eating honey-roasted peanuts.

If the plane is going down, the only flotation device appropriate is a parachute. Frankly, the Federal Aviation Administration (FAA) should consider requiring parachutes on commercial flights, especially on late-night "red-eye" flights. It is surprising that neither Congress nor the FAA haven't already passed a law requiring that parachutes be issued to passengers prone to sleepwalking.

The FAA, or perhaps even someone with the National Transportation Safety Board (NTSB), should coordinate a public information campaign about how recycled air works. This effort should be targeted to those ridiculous folks who, upon clambering aboard the plane, immediately kick off their shoes in the name of comfort. If smoking is no longer allowed on domestic flights, flying shoeless should also be prohibited. If we don't want to intrude on the freedom of in-flight shoe removers, fine. Issue them Ziplock bags for their feet, or booties like doctors wear in surgery.

> "Since airlines seem to lack a 'No Shoes, No Shirt, No Service' policy, why not divide planes into sections like in restaurants? Ticket agents could ask 'Stocking or non?'"

Don't misunderstand -- I am not anti-foot. Quite the contrary, I have two feet of my own. I never metatarsal I didn't like and, in fact, I even worship western footwear. I am a bootist. Our congregation isn't large but we've got sole. Sometimes we pray for the sick to heel.

Since airlines seem to lack a "No Shoes, No Shirt, No Service" policy, why not divide planes into sections like in restaurants? Ticket agents could ask "Stocking or non?" All the footloose and fancy-free types should sit in the back of the plane near the restrooms, keeping their funky feet to themselves. Conversely, those of us with the dignity and self-control to keep our shoes on for the whole ride could be rewarded by being allowed to deplane more quickly.

If Congress passed such legislation, it would have widespread national support. Members of Congress should begin drafting legislation on this important issue because America is ready for "Foot Bill" season. It may sound crazy, but trust me -- such a bill has a good chance of passage. Better than campaign finance reform, anyway.

As for the grass strip runway in Nebraska, we landed without incident and I did the "gig." However, I made a point of making sure my return flight had a movie and real snack. Even though it didn't have parachutes or booties, two out of four isn't bad.

Water Purification, the Old-Fashioned Way

*W*ater-quality issues have been in the news quite a bit lately. Several years ago, Washington, D.C., was lambasted for having unhealthy levels of lead. Skinny guys like me welcome lead-filled water. It is cheaper than the overpriced WeightGainer available through Muscle and Fitness magazine, and it seems to do the same job. I may set off metal detectors at the airport, but at least I'm putting on weight. Best of all, it's free. Unfortunately, many communities have water problems that are more serious.

To wit: Medicine Bow, Wyoming, like so many other small rural towns across the country, added chlorine to its water in July, 1997, after tests by the Environmental Protection Agency (EPA) showed it to be rife with coliform bacteria. The bacteria, much like the EPA itself, is not life-threatening but has been shown to give people headaches. Complying with the orders, Medicine Bow Mayor Gerald Cook pumped Clorox bleach into the town's water system. The chlorine would not only kill the bacteria but also would help clothes look their whitest.

According to the Wyoming Association of Rural Water Systems, Clorox is the standard for giving "shock treatment" to the bacteria. Because of the vast amount of water involved, the bleach is diluted to the point where it is not harmful to humans. This is especially bad news to coffee drinkers who were counting on the bleach to whiten their teeth.

Unfortunately, bleaching the bugs into submission is at best a temporary solution. I am hardly an expert but I have done laundry a number of times and believe I know what I am talking about. For example, after bleaching discolored parts of my undershirts, I am frequently saddened to discover that, weeks later, the shirts *again* look like I've had earwax in a headlock. Thusly, Medicine Bow's water problem could occur again. "All it takes is a couple of little bits of dirt getting in the (water) lines somewhere," Town Clerk Carol Cook told an Associated Press reporter.

Communities have been adding chemicals to their water for

years. Fluoride was introduced to local water supplies decades ago to make teeth more resistant to cavities and decay. According to rumor, many prisons used to add saltpeter to their water supply to create a more placid inmate population – until it was deemed cruel and unusual to drug inmates without their consent. Experts point out such policies are less than stringent and feature many exceptions. Lethal injections, for example.

> "With caffeinated tapwater, Sanka might actually help people wake up in the morning."

It's frustrating that communities like Medicine Bow aren't putting *MORE* additives in their water. Now that grocery stores are carrying caffeinated water -- bottled water spiked with the same amount of caffeine found in coffee -- I am surprised that towns nationwide haven't tried to perk up their residents. Imagine the benefits! A more alert citizenry would yield fewer traffic accidents, as well as a workforce capable of working longer hours. It would be a new Golden Age! Better yet, folks could cook with caffeinated water, leading to caffeinated pasta, caffeinated Jell-O and even caffeinated decaffeinated coffee! With caffeinated tapwater, Sanka might actually help people wake up in the morning.

For years, ever since the town drilled a new well that was contaminated with radium, the EPA has had Medicine Bow under surveillance. As everyone who took basic chemistry knows, radium is radioactive and is thought to be among the causes of Godzilla, Mothra and Ross Perot's ears. Be that as it may, a solution to Medicine Bow's radium-tainted water seems obvious: mix its water with D.C.'s lead-filled water. Everytime they blanket you with that 80-pound vest before zapping you with x-rays, dentists remind us that lead absorbs radiation. They also say that x-rays can't harm you, right before diving into the hall where it's safe.

Communities like Medicine Bow, Wyoming, and Washington, D.C., should work together to ensure safer water for everybody. Such an arrangement would mean the end of my free lead-based WeightGainer tapwater but it is a small price to pay to ensure that small town America has safe, radiation-free water to drink.

Now, if only Clorox could be persuaded to develop a line of flavored bleaches.

Kall It "Ku Klux Kompliance"

It goes without saying that the Ku Klux Klan, like the U.S. Senate, has long been a bastion of white men who wish to remain anonymous -- the original "boys in the hood," as it were. While the United States moves ever closer to racial harmony, the embittered Klan continues to survive through Klan-related merchandisers who sell white supremacist paraphernalia -- ersatz "white sales" -- at rallies, conventions and the occasional Denny's restaurant.

In spite of the Klan's new websites and other technical innovations, the multi-million dollar group, based in the South, is taking heat for its refusal to change with the times. Adding insult to racially-motivated injury, the group is being scrutinized by governmental regulators for failing to comply with various federal regulations.

As a "not-for-profit" organization, the Klan receives tax-exempt status similar to that of the March of Dimes, Greenpeace and the B'Nai Brith. Such groups fall under section 501(c)3 of the U.S. Tax Code. Some suggest the beleaguered Warner Brothers Network falls into this category, but a spokesman clarified: "The fact that we are unprofitable doesn't mean we are a not-for-profit."

Because refusal to comply with U.S. tax laws may result in the rescission of one's tax-exempt status, some believe the Klan should participate in affirmative action as a show of good faith. Either that, or risk having to pay the dreaded Internal Revenue Service each year.

Proponents of affirmative action believe the role of the federal government is to ensure the freedom and rights of all citizens in a way that does not separate, discriminate or show favoritism to any specific group of people. "As we enter the 21st century," said an IRS spokesperson, "hiring people of color will be a good way for the Klan to diversify its workforce and improve its organizational culture."

> "Hiring people of color will be a good way for the Klan to diversify its workforce and improve its organizational culture."

In addition, the Klan currently faces challenges from a variety of governmental agencies. The supremacist group currently is fighting the Environmental Protection Agency, who charges that the group's reliance on burning crosses and arson-related acts only compounds America's problems with air pollution and contributes to global warming.

Equally litigious is the Occupational Safety and Health Administration (OSHA) who contends that cross burnings and other acts of arson require the use of "flame-retardant clothing, appropriate gloves and safety eyewear," none of which were noted in a recent OSHA inspection of the Klan's main office. Required use of hoods, or other clothing that may be harmful to the wearer by inhibiting normal breathing, may also violate OSHA rules.

As for promoting equality through affirmative action, "The Klan has always been dedicated to equality," said a hooded Klan spokesman. "We hate everybody equally. We hate the hoods and robes too but, most of all, we hate people like OSHA who don't respect our traditions." Negotiations between the Klan and the IRS are ongoing. Sources say the KKK will agree to add African kente cloth to their robes if they are allowed to hire people of color only for entry level jobs, and if noted Klansmen Daniel Carver and David Duke are allowed to make guest appearances on an episode of "Moesha." No word yet on whether this is agreeable to the IRS but, with April 15th fast approaching, time is of the essence!

Tooth or Dare

*B*elieve it or not, letting your teeth rot from Halloween candy might save your life. Dentists agree, though they won't admit it. After all, holiday sweets are the only things keeping dentists in business these days. Thanks to fluoride in municipal water supplies, the number of cavities is on the decline. This is why, off the record, most dentists will encourage you to use bottled water -- it has no fluoride. The less fluoride in your mouth, the more you will need the manhandling known as dental work.

Dentists won't deny that candy is chock full of dental-visit goodness. Tangy Taffy and Brach's caramel cubes are also industry favorites, as each piece wraps around each tooth and won't let go until washed away by carbonated soda. The combined effect is the dentist's crowning achievement -- guaranteed customers in an otherwise orally-hygienic society.

Clearly, a child's best hope is to get dentures. Dentures don't get cavities so the amount of candy that can be eaten is virtually limitless. Moreover, dentures go well with "wax lips," a staple of both candy fans and those too cheap to pay for collagen injections. Having a mouth full of false teeth may not sound glamorous but many celebrities have them, including hockey players, boxers, and guests on "The Jerry Springer Show."

Even President George Washington had false teeth because he knew that brushing one's teeth is potentially hazardous to one's health. If you don't believe the Father of Our Country, read the back of your toothpaste tube. You likely will find a poison label that you may not have noticed before: "If you accidentally swallow more than used for brushing, seek professional help or contact a poison control center immediately."

The Food and Drug Administration (FDA) currently requires toothpaste manufacturers to include poison labeling on all fluoride toothpastes and dental care products. Before April 7, 1997, when the FDA requirement went into effect, toothpastes carried only simple suggestions. Familiar ones include "Don't swallow -- use

21

only a pea-sized amount for children under 6" or "Children under 6 should be supervised while brushing with any toothpaste to prevent swallowing."

As reported by the Washington Post, Regina Miskewitz, director of research and development for oral and personal care at Church and Dwight Co., Inc., -- the maker of Arm & Hammer products -- says three ingredients in toothpaste pose health risks if too much is ingested. Sorbitol, a liquid that keeps toothpaste from drying out, is a laxative that can cause "complications" in small children. Sodium laurel sulfate, the ingredient that makes toothpaste foam, is similarly problematic. Of the three, however, fluoride is the most dangerous if swallowed -- particularly among younger children. "Small amounts of this material go a long way in causing disruption in their bodies because they are so small," Miskewitz told reporters.

> "Instead of holiday sweets, parents should think about giving their kids an appointment with a prosthodontist."

A 1995 study at the Medical College of Georgia School of Dentistry found that about half the children aged 4-6 years old don't spit or rinse out after brushing. Instead, they swallow the toothpaste. "That's why it's recommended that kids only get a pea-size amount of toothpaste," Miskewitz added. "Most of that goes down their throats." Worse, kids tend to use too much toothpaste if left unsupervised, especially when using novelty-flavored toothpastes.

Instead of holiday sweets, parents should think about giving their kids an appointment with a prosthodontist. By giving children false teeth early in life, parents can avoid having to invest in braces, retainers and wisdom teeth removal, and spare candy makers from layoffs. As a favor to your dentist, don't brush your teeth.

Now, if you'll excuse me, I am late for a dental appointment. If I'm good, the dentist might give me a lollipop.

Business is Booming for UNICOR

*U*ntil his transfer to another federal facility in July 1999, noted baby boomer Timothy McVeigh and acclaimed writer Ted Kaczynski enjoyed time together in Florence, Colorado, in a federal prison called "The Big One." Each had his own room in the "Alcatraz of the Rockies," though each was thought to be unhappy. Experts fear their "single-cell anemia" might have been cured by allowing the two to room together. The two have a great deal in common and surely would have had a bang-up time.

Though they no longer live under the same roof, Kaczynski and McVeigh might yet be enlisted in UNICOR, the corporation run by Federal Prison Industries. Administered by the U.S. Bureau of Prisons, UNICOR began in 1934 as a way to teach inmates marketable job skills. Because "busy hands are happy hands," as the old saying goes, the program has far outstripped the image of working on license plates and laundry.

In 1997, UNICOR employed 18,414 federal inmates and produced $512.8 million in catalogued goods and services made for, and sold to, the U.S. government. It also deposited more than $1.8 million in the Inmate Financial Responsibility Program, which funds family support, court-ordered fines and victims' restitution.

UNICOR could help Kaczynski and McVeigh keep their job skills sharp, while expanding the portfolio of services produced by federal inmates. Through inmates at 72 federal prisons, UNICOR produces hundreds of millions of dollars worth of pajamas, desk chairs, and various products for the federal government and other high-volume purchasers.

Why let the specialized expertise of Kaczynski and McVeigh go to waste? As experienced as the two are with explosives, UNICOR could win defense contracts as a supplier of munitions and ordnance and possibly enter the commercial demolitions market.

Governmental demolitions are occasionally needed, too. Like those big hotels in Las Vegas and skyscrapers in New York, federal buildings occasionally need to be imploded to improve public safety. The U.S. Capitol, for example, has been standing for more than 200 years. "Buildings that old are just accidents waiting to happen," said John Doe #2, a confidant of McVeigh, who went on to say McVeigh's dedication to safety was epitomized by a selfless act of personally-financed demolition in Oklahoma City in 1995. Point taken. When one considers the cost of the Ryder truck and fertilizer involved, jobs that size aren't cheap.

> "According to sources, [Kaczynski] is said to be a real pro when it comes to targeted mailings."

In addition to demolition work, Kaczynski could assist UNICOR's ongoing telemarketing efforts. According to sources, he is said to be a real pro when it comes to targeted mailings. The most UNICOR pays any inmate is $1.12 an hour. "With postage rates on the rise," said a source, "Kaczynski could really use the money."

True enough. Sales of his writings are down, which is surprising considering the buzz created by his first opus, "Manifesto." His follow-up, a cookbook entitled "Cooking for One: The Rustic Recipes of the UnaChef," features the down-home goodness of Montana's outback cuisine. Single guys living without electricity will have a blast with his recipes for turnips, carrots and other garden favorites. The book also features several chapters on the folly of over-reliance on technology, and a special "Did You Know...?" trivia section for kids.

Many labor union officials and industry groups are concerned about UNICOR, and believe the use of prison labor results in unfair competition and takes jobs away from law-abiding workers. Because many prisoners work for little or no compensation, some call prison labor a new form of slavery. Others disagree, and believe that Kaczynski and McVeigh are free -- free to make cheaper, more reliable explosives for the military, or government demolition efforts. America's economy is booming and it is high time prison economies were, too.

Smoke 'Em If You Got 'Em

*N*ot long ago, smokes were a de facto currency in our nation's prisons. However, lawsuits from non-smoking inmates have prompted the Occupational Safety and Health Administration (OSHA), as well as the Bureau of Prisons (BOP) and various other agencies charged with protecting the nation's prison inmates, to ban smoking in most prisons from California to Massachusetts. For example, in Bucks County, Pennsylvania, a ban came after a union filed a grievance in 1997 claiming tobacco-fouled air was responsible for the headaches and sinus problems of workers.

Wardens in non-smoking facilities report their prisoners are getting healthier and jails are becoming more hygienic. However, many inmates are calling the "clean air" policies cruel and unusual because smoking bans prevent inmates from lighting up after sex.

Because modern prisons don't have windows that open and, instead, rely on recirculated air systems, the problems associated with 500 people smoking indoors 24 hours a day is not hard to imagine. The cumulative effects of such conditions are comparable to each prison employee chain-smoking two cartons of Dorals, or bowling three games with Rep. John Boehner (R-Ohio) in the R.J. Reynolds Invitational Bowl-a-thon at Virginia Slims Lanes in Winston-Salem, North Carolina.

Besides cleaner air, supporters of tobacco-free prison environments point to fewer burn holes in clothing and bedding, fewer fires and a reduced need to paint over yellowing walls. Ironically, some members of the health profession worry that the practice of banning cigarettes actually harms drug-addicted inmates. This may explain why some soft-hearted prison guards are willing to "import" cigarettes for cash. As a practical measure, the Georgia Department of Corrections repealed its smoking ban after prisoners brawled over contraband cigarettes selling for $20 a pack.

Despite a black market of illegally imported tobacco products, the Associated Press reported on January 28, 1998, that the supply of tobacco smokes has steadily dwindled in many prisons. As a result, in some cases, the price of one cigarette is as high as five boxes of Little Debbie snack cakes.

At $2.20 per box, tea bags are also an increasingly popular smoking substitute. However, with rising prices for such luxury items, many inmates are resorting to grass clippings, orange rinds, or apple peels wrapped in toilet paper. Nicotine patches don't seem to have caught on in prison -- probably because they are so hard to keep lit. One may safely assume the same is true of Nicorette gum.

> "Frankly, if one is doing a life sentence, who wants to be healthy?"

Frankly, if one is doing a life sentence, who wants to be healthy? Living longer only means longer incarceration and more punishment. Also, it means more license plates, more breaking of rock, more annoying cellmates and, lest we forget, more communal showering. For these reasons, giving cigarettes to lifers and death row inmates may be among the most humane things our civilized society can do for those who are incarcerated. Also, flooding prisons with cigarettes gives tobacco farmers, still reeling from last year's crippling ban on child-oriented marketing, a fighting chance. In this manner, America's economy will remain the strongest in the world while concerns about overcrowded prisons will go up in smoke.

Put Class Back In The Classroom

*E*ach August, parents across the nation count the days until kids head back to school. Unfortunately, many parents are guilty on two counts of undermining the nation's education system -- by letting their children choose what they will wear to school and by being sub par "fashion role-models."

Despite the severity of these problems, Congress has shown only slight interest in them by focusing instead on such things as vouchers for private education, outcomes-based curricula and the menace of Attention Deficit/Hyperactivity Disorder (ADHD). However, no consensus has been reached and the decline of the American public education proceeds apace. To wit: a survey by the U.S. Department of Education and the National Assessment of Educational Progress in 1997 revealed that 57 percent of high school seniors performed below basic levels of proficiency.

Instead of blaming the nation's education establishment, some suggest American students *deserve* such scores. Parents and teachers alike complain that students seem to take little pride in their appearance, which is reflected in the quality of their schoolwork. Psychologists say these are symptoms of low self-esteem and pronounced social apathy. Sure, the kids look like hoboes but I argue that today's kids are every bit as fashion-conscious as previous generations.

For example, kids spend more on those flannel-shirt and baggy-pants ensembles than some teachers do on their mortgages. That greasy crewcut? $70 at The Look. The cheap flannel shirt? $110 at Abercrombie and Fitch. Accoutrements, like those crummy construction boots that used to cost $22 at Payless or $15 at Wheelers, will top $100 as well. Add in the cost of novelty boxer shorts, which have to be exactly right since they spend half their time peering out the top of Junior's half-mast baggy pants -- et voila! "Hobo" by Ralph Lauren. Frankly, we should not be surprised that modern students dress like Beverly Hillbillies 90210 because adults encourage it each and every "Casual Friday."

Congress and the U.S. Department of Education should consider the possibility that poor academic performance, and any associated lack of self-esteem among students, may come from teachers and parents themselves. More specifically, students are being desensitized to the need for proper appearance by grown-ups increasingly fond of Casual Fridays and school psychologists who recklessly promote "being in touch with one's Inner Child." Both must stop because, sooner or later, the Inner Child will need to get a job in the Outer World. On a recent fact-finding mission to a public school, I learned -- to my horror -- that finding a necktie on male faculty members is as difficult as finding students who haven't done drugs by the age of 14.

> "To end the root rot that is an increasingly lax faculty dress code, 'Tuxedo Fridays' might be something to encourage."

"Dressing less like an authority figure and more like a friend," as one school psychologist put it, is on the rise. Faculty members of public schools may soon defend Casual Semesters with a plaintive "I wear bunny slippers to class because I teach better when I am comfortable" and the utilitarian "I'm doing it for the kids!" This specious reasoning may work in home schools but, in public schools, relaxed attire should be limited to Physical Education departments before it infects the detail-oriented curricula of math, science and grammar. Professional educators should be more aware of the example they set and work to end the root rot that is an increasingly lax faculty dress code. "Tuxedo Fridays" might be something to encourage. Spats – they're not just for marching band anymore!

Congress, state legislatures and school boards would do well to hold hearings on this issue. The U.S. Department of Education should be invited to testify on what is being done to guard against the plague of Casual Semesters. Leading educators or the Secretary of Education should be questioned about what plans, if any, are afoot to improve declining fashions in public schools. Another item to discuss might be that, with an increasingly technical workplace,

Wood Shop courses should be given art credits instead of vocational education credits. Building a spice rack or a butter churn is not the lucrative industry it once was. In fact, the market is pretty bleak, unless one plans on living among the Amish to churn butter or make spice racks for tourists.

We should stop placing blame for poor academic performance and falling post-high school employment rates on students and their families. It is high time that teachers and parents faced the reality that they must cooperate to inspire more than rote learning. This next school year, look for Tuxedo Fridays -- coming to a classroom near you!

Home Sweet Floating Home

*F*or generations, great minds always have been assaulted by conventional wisdom and popular opinion. Centuries ago, for example, Leonardo DaVinci invented a parachute. Of course, he sold very few -- not only because aircraft hadn't yet been invented but also because his parachute was simply the steeple from a local building and tended to crush the parachutists shortly after landing. As a result, DaVinci's sales plummeted at a rate of 32.2 feet per second squared.

Through the years, the spirit of invention has moved us ever forward. All humility aside, I am among these great minds and believe strongly that my idea for Tupperware housing will save innumerable lives -- particularly in earthquake-prone areas and flood plains. An obvious criticism is that, each summer, Tupperware houses would have to be "burped." Burping notwithstanding, such homes would have many advantages; they wouldn't break apart in earthquakes, they would float in floods and they would keep personal possessions cool and crisp. I may be crazy like a fox but, unfortunately, I'm not original like one.

Paul Winston, a builder of modular homes in Englewood, Colorado, conceived, designed and received a patent for his "Winston Land-Locked Floating House" in less than 190 days in 1993. That's pretty fast, as such things go. The U.S. Patent and Trademark Office believed the idea unusual -- but practical -- and of great potential benefit to homebuyers in traditionally flood-prone areas.

In essence, his design works like this: as floodwaters surround the house, the water pushes against a series of buoyant rectangular plastic tubs filled with urethane foam placed beneath the building. The upward pressure causes telescoping steel-pipe supports -- like the kind used in deep-sea oil-drilling rigs, only smaller -- to extend from anchored wooden pilings, lifting the house and attached two-car garage by as much as 20 feet.

A thermostat-like device regulates ballast, with sensors and pumps automatically letting water in or forcing it out to keep the house on an even keel. The house is anchored to one spot by being permanently tied to four telescoping steel piers. Utilities would be attached with flexible connectors designed to break and shut off automatically if floodwaters push the house too high. Winston told reporters that computer modeling shows his design will not only withstand strong water currents but winds of up to 120 mph as well.

Unfortunately, Winston hasn't gotten a *flood* of interest from the Federal Emergency Management Agency (FEMA) -- the government's lead flood control agency. Despite support from the Army Corps of Engineers, the Department of Housing and Urban Development (HUD), Lloyd's of London and Members of Congress -- including Sens. Patty Murray (D-Wash.), Christopher "Kit" Bond (R-Mo.) and Connie Mack (R-Fla.) -- if FEMA doesn't want a Floating House, no other agency will test the design nor buy it.

> "Tupperware housing was my idea first."

In spite of legislation which passed in 1994 instructing FEMA to be accommodating in testing new technologies which may provide feasible means of flood-proofing residential structures in flood-prone areas, Winston is still struggling upstream against the rapids of the federal bureaucracy.

Thankfully, Congress is continuing to look into this matter. It would be a tragedy for America -- indeed, for the spirit of invention -- to leave innovative ideas from small businesspeople stuck in dry dock like this. Of course, it will also be a tragedy if Winston makes a fortune from his Floating House idea and doesn't share any of it with me. After all, Tupperware housing was my idea first.

Modern Parents "Just Say Ritalin"

*E*ach year, when school lets out for another summer, parents of children with short attention spans -- the advocates of Attention Deficit/Hyperactivity Disorder (ADHD) -- are among those crossing their fingers and hoping for relief. Ever since the dawn of time, ADHD was not a medical condition. Instead, it was commonly known as "having ants in the pants" or "being the class clown." This affliction is not limited to hyperactive schoolchildren. Many hardworking members of Congress are afflicted by this nightmarish disease, like Sen. Connie Mack (R-Fla.). Why else would he use the abbreviated version of his family name -- Cornelius McGillicuddy? Some experts speculate that the rise in media soundbites, governmental acronyms and hemlines on television programs are related to the rise in ADHD.

In 1996, the General Accounting Office (GAO) reported that the Social Security Administration (SSA) has done a poor job of following up on the status of the estimated 135,000 children who receive ADHD-related benefits. The report used powerful phrases like "ripe for fraud and abuse," "checks have been erroneously sent" and that the SSA "pays benefits to too many people for too long." Investigations like the GAO's inspire many politicians to wonder whether there is a continued need for such funding, or if it will continue to be plagued with administrative problems and misdiagnosis.

Fearful that the federal gravy train may be leaving the station, numerous parent groups -- spurred forth by child care professionals like school psychologists -- continue to ask the government to fund Expensive Medical Research to find a cure for this dread affliction.

Of course, when word of Expensive Medical Research spreads through the scientific community, it is like ringing Pavlov's bell. The drooling of white-smocked researchers sounds like rain on hot concrete -- and especially so for ADHD studies. Scientists would not only have permission but a *mandate* to exact revenge on class clowns for years of teasing in junior high school.

> "An entire way of life died the day Congress considered ADHD a medically-legitimate illness."

Practices like flushing a geek's head in the toilet between classes, and comments like "Hey four-eyes," "Hey nerd," and "You look like Al Gore" will come to an end if the ADHD bandwagon has its way. An entire way of life died the day Congress considered ADHD a medically-legitimate illness.

According to sources, the National Institutes of Health (NIH) eagerly await conducting such studies, which are said to require the vivisection of hand-picked domesticated class clowns reflecting an even geographic distribution. Surely, the funny bone will be the first thing to be studied, amid cries of "You're not so funny NOW, are you Billy Mahoney?" and "This is what you get for always locking me in my gym locker!" For many aging class clowns, the time of retribution is at hand.

Social workers, schoolteachers and other professionals with equally dubious pharmacological training suggest that drugging class clowns into submission with Ritalin is the prudent course of action. Not only does Ritalin permit children to continue their studies without the nuisance of stitches or time lost due to funnybonectomies, the drug also allows school districts to further their agendas of turning happy-go-lucky individuals into mind-controlled zombies. Thanks to Ritalin, school districts achieve in students by the age of 12 what the real world normally accomplishes by the age of 30.

Ironically, parents in favor of drugging their children with Ritalin tend to oppose putting saltpeter in school water systems to reduce the sexual urges of students. Apparently, parents are comfortable with promiscuous children on drugs so long as they are mild-mannered and boring.

In any event, it is clear that Nancy Reagan's "Just Say No!" effort has been undermined by a "Just Say Ritalin!" campaign waged by ill-informed parents and overzealous school psychologists. Thanks to their efforts, the class clown is dead.

Long live the class clown.

A Rose Is a Rose Is a Jeffrey Dahmercopter

*W*hile Congress wrings its collective hands in concern about ethical lapses, and points toward the vacuum of moral leadership in the White House, attention is being directed away from other problems. One such matter is the way in which many Native Americans are misrepresented by the degrading or ignorant use of their names or cultures.

For example, a Libertarian Party news release dated February 19, 1999, reported that Erwin High School in Asheville, North Carolina, was under investigation by the U.S. Department of Justice for the school's sports team -- the Warriors. If certain civil rights violations are associated with Erwin High School's mascot, which some feel is culturally-insensitive, the school risked nearly $8 million in fines.

This is not a new concern, of course. For years, many have discussed the cultural abuse inherent in deriving sports teams from the Native American heritage. The Crazy Horse Defense Project, a not-for-profit group organized to encourage portraying native Americans in a more positive light, cite the Washington Redskins, the Cleveland Indians, the Atlanta Braves, the Kansas City Chiefs, the Florida State Seminoles, the University of Utah Utes and the Chicago Blackhawks as examples of outright cultural insensitivity. These concerns are understandable but, frankly, there are bigger issues at stake. Rather than focus on the proliferation of Native American-themed sports team names, attention must be paid to a larger abuser of cultural heritage: the government itself.

The federal government, specifically the U.S. Department of Defense (DOD), has been in the business of cultural abuse for many years, scavenging through the Native American heritage to give intimidating names to its tools of death and destruction. Do not misunderstand -- I am a strong supporter of military readiness, as I am of maintaining our country's presence on the world stage. However, I disagree with naming military weapons after Native Americans because of the stigma it perpetuates.

The Cheyenne Nation ought to be furious about the infamous Cheyenne Mountain in Colorado, housing the North American Air Defense (NORAD) complex that controls the nation's nuclear response systems. Additionally, assault helicopters like the "Apache," the "Iroquois," the "Cayuse," the "Blackhawk" and the "Kiowa," not to mention the "Tomahawk" cruise missile, are all capable of pacifying America's enemies and inflicting substantial collateral damage. All well and good, these devices were designed to do a certain job and it is comforting that they are on our side. However, giving Native American names to such devices is disconcerting, to say the least.

If intimidation is what American military weapons and vehicles are designed to do, why not use more appropriate nomenclature? This calls to mind the argument of whether or not the clothes make the man. In this instance, do the names make the weapons? I think not. An armored assault helicopter will savage the enemy just as well called a "Petunia" or even a "Richard Simmons." A rose is a rose is a rose. However, friends in the military tell me that such names would never meet military specifications (milspecs) because the psychology of warfare demands that weapons have intimidating names. Fine.

> "Arm helicopters with 50-calibre Ted Kaczynski machine guns and a few Son of Sam missiles."

Trouble in Kosovo? Why not send over a group of O.J. Simpson-class helicopters, each armed with 50-calibre Ted Kaczynski machine guns and a few Son of Sam missiles. What's that? There is unrest in Bosnia? Dispatch a wing of Jeffrey Dahmercopters and tell the pilots to unleash their Manson-tipped JacktheRippers. If that is insufficient, a couple of Joe Camel B-1Bs could dump loads of Frandreschers on them. While Fran Drescher, TV's "The Nanny," hasn't officially killed anyone, those who saw "The Beautician and the Beast" will agree it was a bomb worthy of its own military designation.

It is my fervent hope that the DOD will take these suggestions to heart and adopt more appropriate names for military weaponry.

The government has a long record of making things difficult for Native Americans, so let us work to free their heritage from continued affiliation with death and mass destruction. Afterwards, Erwin High School could name its sports teams whatever it wants. For the record, I think the "Johnwaynegacies" is the team name to beat. With a name like that, Erwin High School surely would BURY their opposition.

Politics and Government

"I don't make jokes. I just watch the government and report the facts."

-- Will Rogers, American humorist

Human Guinea Pigging: The Next Capitol Punishment?

My grandfather once said nothing is sure except debt and taxes. Cynicism notwithstanding, the point is sound. As the snows of winter retreat, America's mind turns to one thing: MONEY. Questions like "How am I going to pay my taxes?" and "How am I going to pay my campaign debts?" emerge like spring flowers.

Finding it more legally bothersome to host impromptu fundraisers nowadays, Members of Congress needing some fast cash should consider an increasingly popular alternative: Paid Medical Experimentation. Due to dust-covered laws in dire need of changing, it is illegal in the United States to traffic in body parts -- which is why Michael Jackson goes to Switzerland for cosmetic surgery. As a result of such archaic laws, human guinea pigs are constantly sought by medical researchers.

Due to high demand and a comparatively small percentage of the human populace willing to submit to medical experiments, researchers often pay top dollar. Since funds generated from being a human guinea pig are exempted from the "outside income" guidelines of Congress, this windfall would be especially helpful to Members of Congress who owe the federal government millions for failed congressional and presidential bids.

Medical experimentation would be of unquestionable financial assistance. Also, for those members with an eye towards future races, human guinea pigging would provide numerous photo opportunities. Members of Congress supportive of efforts to cure cancer, AIDS and other illnesses would rocket skyward in the polls due to their efforts to personally lead the fight toward finding a cure.

In addition, clones made from Scottish sheep and, in Oregon, rhesus pieces have sparked new interest in the field of genetics. My contacts in the British Embassy are not enthused with the high-tech sheep and inform me that Dolly was cloned as part of a project to increase the world's haggis supply. In any event, congressional funding for cloning research is likely to be generous.

Believing we are on the Eve of an era where it is possible to split the Adam, many members are interested in cloning themselves as a source of free campaign labor. Senator Robert Byrd (D-W. Va.) reportedly plans to make a back-up "Billie," the pointless shaggy-dog stories of which could fill the Congressional Record past the lifespan of the original. It is interesting that the White House is opposed to such experimentation, as cloning could do more to create Democrat voters than the failed "Citizenship USA" program, and could create additional Al Gores who could each raise campaign funds while "Alpha" Gore does his job searching for controlling legal authority.

Genetics research will impact the private sector as well. It is not difficult to envision a future where Main Street, America, is lined with "I Can't Believe It's Not A Sperm Bank!" and "Boys R Us." In record numbers, women are profiting from genetics research by selling their eggs. The question of whether women should profit from their bodies in this manner has yet to be answered, as some suggest that "ova the counter" sales demean women by reducing them to little more than egg cartons.

The same could be asked about men who sell sperm at fertility clinics. President Clinton appointed a task force to look into the "bio-ethics" of sperm banks and related facilities and it may not be long before he seeks funding, if not a Cabinet seat, for a Federal Erection Commission. Former Senator Bob Packwood (R-Ore.) has time on his hands and surely would be available to serve as chair. The President should not waste this historic opportunity! The savvy Member of Congress will run, not walk, to the nearest fertility clinic to make a "contribution" to genetics research (photo op optional) and put the proceeds to use in their War Chest.

The downside to this novel debt repayment plan is that the genetic material of some Members of Congress could be in a fertility clinic near you! Due to the rising cost of elections, be on the lookout -- an indebted Member of Congress could be the father of YOUR next child!

Spelling Errors are National Traditoin

*F*or those who have ever taken flak for occasional spelling errors, take heart: you are not alone. Typos are the natural result of America's pronounced use of abbreviations. From ESPN and "The X-Games," to C-SPAN and "The X-Files," abbreviations and acronyms are in conspicuous abundance across the USA.

Government agencies earn them with lengthy names, like the National Institute of Arthritis and Musculoskeletal and Skin Diseases (NIAMSD). Long after President Richard Nixon's Committee to Reelect the President (CREEP), security arrangements for the highest levels of American government continue to revolve around the POTUS (President of the United States) and the FLOTUS (First Lady of the United States). However, folks are encouraged to spell their names out when writing campaign donation checks. Modern political efforts rely on acronyms, like President Gerald Ford's campaign to "Whip Inflation Now" (WIN), as do political action committees like former House Speaker Newt Gingrich's "GOPAC." While no elected officials have yet referred to the Constitution of the United States as "COTUSA," give it time.

As many know, modern employers are reluctant to hire those who can't spell, in spite of the availability of software like SpellCheck and Grammatik designed to help people overcome this disability. Though the Americans with Disabilities Act does not yet protect the "spelling-impaired," that day is coming. Imagine – not needing to spell AND getting a good parking space! Truly, the good times are yet to come.

The rise in abbreviations may reflect the American fear of spelling errors. Of course, by "spelling errors," I am not referring to television shows on the Fox Network by Aaron Spelling. Not entirely, anyway. Typographical errors are honest, albeit humbling, mistakes but they are not unique to the 20th century. In fact, many can be found in the Constitution itself. Want to have some fun and teach your children more about the frailties of our Founding Fathers? Here's a suggestion: proofread the Constitution.

> "Modern bellmakers know that SpellCheck is a great help to their industry, and give it a *ringing* endorsement."

Every American should know that the Liberty Bell has a typo on it, as do all copies thereof. The bell's spelling of Pennsylvania has one too few N's but, in fairness, some believe the Liberty Bell's famous crack wouldn't be there if only Wite-Out had existed in colonial times. Modern bellmakers know that SpellCheck is a great help to their industry, and give it a *ringing* endorsement. During your next scheduled family time, emphasize to your children that if they don't study their spelling, sociologists and satirists in the future will make fun of them. American children can be excused if they have a hard time remembering exactly what is on the Liberty Bell, who was at Pickett's Charge or even where the Siege of Corinth was. The wealth of spelling errors throughout Americana is more than a little distracting.

To reiterate, the Constitution -- our most hallowed governmental document -- is riddled with spelling errors. Rather than a Balanced Budget Amendment, Congress should consider a "SpellCheck the Constitution" Amendment. Aside from words like "defence" and "offence," which reflect the English-derived spellings at the time, and a smattering of inappropriately capitalized words in the middle of sentences, there are many typos throughout the Constitution.

No amendments have any spelling errors, which is a comfort. A fun game on your family's next vacation might be "Let's Count the Typos in the Constitution!" How many times does the word "chuse" appear? Six. How about the word "chusing?" Four. The word "labour" appears three times, "behaviour" twice, and "Controul" and "encreased" can be found only once each. If we venture out into grammatical errors, Article 1, Section 10, Paragraph 2 features a particularly needless little apostrophe. The "it's" in this case should, in fact, be an "its."

Spelling and grammatical errors like these should give lawmakers pause when considering issues related to homeschooling.

For those who aren't aware, most of our Founding Fathers were educated at home by parents or "schoolmarms" who themselves were homeschooled, having had no other choice. The Constitution's numerous spelling errors are proof positive that homeschooling is of dubious value. The real lesson is that Americans should stop using abbreviations and acronyms ASAP. Otherwise, for many, job prospects in the USA will be DOA PDQ. The next time someone gives you trouble about spelling, rest assured that typos are your American right -- they're in the Constitution!

The Wonderland That Is the Library of Congress

*A*s many Americans know, the Library of Congress has it all. I was once told by a tour guide that it is actually the tallest building in the world. Curious, I asked "How so?" to which he replied, "Because it has over a million stories." Apparently, American architecture is still number one.

Thanks to a large grant from the Xerox Foundation, the Library recently exhibited some of the many items in her collection. While only a pitiable handful of the library's more than 111 million treasures are on display at any one time, it is breathtaking nonetheless.

Thanks to a bookish little man claiming to be the "Librarian of Congress," I was offered a sneak peek at many of the items in the library's collection. As we toured and looked around, I was pleasantly surprised to see so many young people using the library for studying and various other academic pursuits. Especially gratifying was seeing a new and extremely young Member of Congress there. Though I wanted to introduce myself, I didn't approach him for fear of interrupting the progress he was making in his coloring book.

Instead, my librarian friend and I went into the back of the Library's colossal exhibit to rummage through its treasures. We saw many pieces of priceless Americana, like President James Buchanan's "Great Expectations" membership card and an autographed script from Sen. Fred Thompson's (R-Tenn.) critically-acclaimed film noir, "Barbarians At the Gate."

Other interesting congressional detritus included a pair of pasties belonging to outdoors enthusiast Fanne Fox (which, frankly, didn't fit me very well), a t-shirt from the "Ted Kennedy for Lifeguard" campaign of 1969, and an original manuscript of a collection of poetry by Secretary of Defense William Cohen (R-Maine) from his days at Bowdoin College. While some of the poems were a little sour, many -- such as the one entitled "A Man From Nantucket" -- were quite engaging. However, it could have done without his Jeff Foxworthy-esque foreword:

"If you dig my poems, you might be a Cohen-head."

> "They should have called it 'The Autobiography of Strom Thurmond' but, when it was written, autos hadn't yet been invented."

In an old cardboard box, I chanced upon a spectacularly old and dusty copy of "The Biography of Strom Thurmond." Truth to tell, it's an autobiography but, when it was written, autos hadn't yet been invented. Apparently, the original hardback version had been kept in the Library of Alexandria but was later destroyed by the Romans. As a result, the Library of Congress was able to acquire only the papyrusback version. Though a little yellowed and brittle, sort of like the august senator himself, the papyrus was in good shape and the original cuneiform was still readable.

I confess to some difficulty in keeping the text from scrolling back together but a couple of well-placed copies of former House Speaker Newt Gingrich's largely unread book "1945" allowed me to skim the parchment with ease. I noticed Thurmond's biography had been signed "To God, My First and Best Intern." The hardback version would have been more fun to read, but the Library of Congress is short on space and four or five stone tablets would take up a good deal of room.

It goes without saying that there are more treasures where these came from, so run -- don't walk -- to your local Library of Congress. However, I can't make you do it. As the great American philosopher Yogi Berra once opined, "If the people don't want to come out to the park, nobody's gonna stop 'em."

If You've Got a Leprous Scab on Your Body --
Picket!

*B*irds of a feather not only flock together, they also protest together. On March 11, 1999, most of the remaining 69 patients at the Gillis W. Long Hansen's Disease Center in Carville, Louisiana, marched in protest of efforts to close the increasingly-obsolete facility.

Carrying signs and calling themselves the "Carville Patients Federation," the facility's residents proclaimed their right to live out their lives at the 330-acre prison that is now their home. Many resided there for decades, since state public health laws forced the detention of all sufferers of leprosy.

Now known as Hansen's disease, leprosy is a bacterial illness that attacks peripheral nerves. About 6,000 Americans have the disease, and about 200 new cases are identified by the Centers for Disease Control each year. Thanks to treatment developed in the late 1940s at the facility by physicians of the U.S. Public Health Service and Daughters of Charity Roman Catholic nuns, leprosy is now controllable -- making the facility a victim of its own success. While the patients didn't originally want to go to the Carville facility, they are now worried that the law will make them leave. Evidently, lepers are reluctant to change their spots.

In 1995, when the facility's $18 million budget was threatened, Rep. Richard Baker (R-La.) introduced a bill to protect the patients and ensure further leprosy research. The law, which passed, offered the patients a tax-free annual stipend of $33,000 and free medical care for Hansen's disease in exchange for leaving the facility. According to HHS, 49 of the 188 patients have already taken advantage of this "buy out." The law also allows the remaining patients to remain at the Center for the rest of their lives, but they are being encouraged to leave within three years in order to turn the facility into a Job Corps site. The White House should take note: even *lepers* don't want anything to do with Job Corps.

> "America listens to celebrities. Look what they've done for spotted owls, global warming, hemp and Tibet."

To help these brittle cajuns, even bush league politicos like me know that innovation -- not picketing -- is called for. To ensure their way of life is preserved, the Center's patients should apply for protection under the Endangered Species Act and have Hollywood celebrities organize a demonstration. As every actor from Alec Baldwin to Ronald Reagan knows, America listens to celebrities for its policy decisions. Look what they've done for spotted owls, global warming, hemp and Tibet.

A Hansen's Disease Natural Habitat and Sanctuary would be just the ticket to protect the Carville Patients Federation from unwelcome encroachment by at-risk youth and Job Corps sitemongers. Ecologists would agree that such encroachment might fragment the patients' delicate backwoods ecosystem and threaten their continued survival. Democrats in Congress should be sympathetic to this expansion of the Endangered Species Act. It would have the added benefit of giving the Nature Conservancy and the Sierra Club something to do.

Conservatives also should back the habitat because, as every Republican since President Teddy Roosevelt has known, the root of the word "conservative" is conserve. At the very least, the patients could get a free airplane ride to Yellowstone National Park -- like Interior Secretary Bruce Babbitt did for the Canadian gray wolves in 1994.

Am I a samaritan for offering the Carville Patients Federation this political strategem? Hardly. I'm just a bird -- a mocking bird, maybe, but a bird nonetheless -- out to help others stay the flock in their natural habitats. So, to those who think the Carville Patients Federation is fighting a losing battle, don't say "leper can't" -- say "leper CAN!"

Midgets Not Short On Campaign Funds

*C*ampaign season is here again, and the political tradition of attending receptions has begun anew. Loosely translated, the word "reception" in Campaignese means "bring your checkbook." One has to make appearances at receptions -- partly to show one's support for noble causes but mostly to get invited to the next one. In fact, there are some women who attend receptions and other galas simply to show off their latest plunging-necklined wardrobes. Wittily, I call them "pomp tarts" which may explain why so few talk to me.

Mainly out of boredom, I attended a traditional reception recently for the American Blind/Mute Association (ABMA). Decorum prevented my questioning their judgement in holding a silent auction where everyone bought things sight unseen -- so I kept my mouth shut. When in Rome, so to speak, do as the mutes do.

In retrospect, I probably should have gone to the reception for the American Midget Association (ama). Though a small organization and short on members, ama dwarfs the Association for People Unable to Abbreviate (Association for People Unable to Abbreviate).

Maybe it was the wine, maybe it was the mime quintet, or maybe it was the dulling nature of the reception itself, but a colleague and I soon began a discussion of the topics of the day. He isn't high on my list of favorites, and it isn't often I welcome the patter of little fetes, but I was bored.

I listened attentively as he ranted that "Miss America 1998" Kate Shindle's crusade to distribute condoms to children is misguided. He's right, of course. In my day, there was a name for girls who gave out condoms and it wasn't Miss America. In response, I explained that the "Home Alone" movies are not innocent tales about love and childhood, but rather insidious training films for anarchists. I pressed on with my argument, despite his assertions that I was "misinformed" or "ignorant." Ignorant like a fox!

The "Home Alone" movies, by glamorizing insubordination, property damage and suburban guerilla tactics, will do for today's youth what "Taxi Driver" did for John Hinckley. It may seem crazy to suggest that Macaulay Culkin is this generation's Travis Bickle but, if the President in 2019 gets hit in the head by a swinging can of paint, falls downstairs into a mousetrap-strewn basement or gets a hot iron dropped on his head, don't come crying to me. Moreover, don't be surprised if the hooligan responsible for the assault saw one, if not all, of the "Home Alone" movies.

> "Since I have numerous ideas I'd been anxious to share with her, I raced over to 'chew the fat' -- a reference to the evening's low-end hors d'oeuvres."

Our conversation ended when I noticed the Secretary of Health and Human Services getting a refill on punch. Because there were a number of ideas I'd been anxious to share with her, I raced over to "chew the fat" -- a reference to the evening's low-end hors d'oeuvres. No wonder the ABMA was hosting a fundraiser.

It had been months since I'd last shared my ideas with the Secretary, so it was nice to have some "face-time" with her again. I reintroduced myself and, within seconds, launched into my plan to make prosthetic limbs for pets. Just as I was revealing my decision to market them as "Faux Paws," our conversation was cut short by thick-necked, dark-suited men claiming to be part of an improbable-sounding group called the "Secret" service. According to police records, this is how my conversations always end with members of the Cabinet.

I held my ground until they picked me up and threw me headlong behind a hush of mimes. The mimes were unable to help me, as they seemed to be locked in invisible boxes of some kind. Clearly, the "Secret" service had gotten to them, too.

After I dusted myself off, I rejoined my colleague from the earlier conversation. In no time at all, we began discussing what a ludicrous-sounding name the "Secret" service is, and hypothesizing about the expense borne by taxpayers to create those invisible, sound-proof mime boxes. By the time we were putting on our coats to leave, we had returned to calling each other misinformed about the White House's vulnerability to "Home Alone" movie watchers.

I despise my colleague but I will undoubtedly see him at the next reception. It's a political tradition, after all.

Soft Money -- the Route of All Evil

For as long as Americans can remember, the financing of campaigns for public office has been questionable. Politicians have long been suspect for taking money that is not deservedly theirs and for the appearance of "huckstering," or saying anything for a buck. Congress and various state legislatures have attempted to achieve meaningful campaign finance reform to bring greater accountability into the rising use of so-called "soft monies" in campaigns. For those new to Beltway vernacular, soft monies are so named because getting them is "not hard." No reforms, however, have been successful and none seem to be on the horizon.

In 1997, Sens. John McCain (R-Ariz.) and Russ Feingold (D-Wisc.) crafted a bipartisan bill to reform campaign financing. The bill was praised by the President and by both sides of the aisle in Congress. Months later, the difficulties of effective campaign finance reform were made evident when Feingold himself revealed he would ignore the bill's fundraising limits in his campaign that year against Rep. Mark Neumann (R-Wisc.).

It is ironic that America believes it is acceptable to give money to charitable groups, PBS, and even church whenever the preacher passes around the collection plate. However, Americans feel morally squeamish whenever a political candidate needs similar financial assistance. It takes a lot of financial assistance to compete against well-funded incumbents. Why is it so difficult for Americans to give money to those individuals we want to represent us in elected office? Elected offices and churches are both charities after a fashion and, according to rumor, both appreciate tax advantages. The question remains: why are we generally supportive of one and not the other? While our weekly $5 or $10 donation to the church collection plate may buy tangible items like new hymn covers or upholstery for pew cushions, it can be argued that one gets more "bang for the buck" by giving to political candidates instead of preachers.

> "Preachers make a lot of speeches, too, giving new meaning to the term 'oral sects.'"

Like politicians, preachers make promises, reinforce the faith of the listener and go about working to make the world a better place. Preachers make a lot of speeches, too, giving new meaning to the term "oral sects." However, for some strange reason, Sunday sermons are readily believed while a politician's campaign promises are immediately derided as impossible to deliver.

Campaign finance reform may be hard to believe but no more so than the story about Jonah in the belly of a whale. Both are hard to swallow yet one has more credibility than the other. While no studies have been done on the subject, there are probably as many huckster preachers in America as there are disingenuous politicians. In this time of great change and unrest in the world, with human needs as numerous as they are, a lack of faith is the last thing we need. We should place as much faith in our elected representatives -- indeed, our whole system of government -- as we do our religious leaders. Both call on your trust and make promises that may or may not come true.

The tragedy of the members of Heaven's Gate who, in 1996, were promised that they were only a purple blanket and a shaved head away from a ride on an invisible spaceship, exemplifies the dangers of blind faith. Members of Congress and the clergy both ask for money at some point so that the "fight for right" can continue. Despite their similarities, Americans still manage to draw a distinction between these social roles.

Faith in our elected officials is needed now more than ever. To make the world a better place, Americans should give candidates the benefit of the doubt and encourage elected officials to do the right thing. Safeguards exist in government, as in churches, to remove those who have violated our trust. We must give faith a chance and give elected officials the benefit of the doubt. Unless meaningful campaign reforms are implemented to crack down on unaccountable or otherwise soft monies, Congress will continue to be more "buy partisan" than bipartisan.

Sin to Win, Politically Speaking

My heart is filled with joy. I am excited beyond words -- because I am finally going to be a Father! Thanks to the Internet and modern theology, I will be ordained as a minister in the next day or so. According to the information on the Universal Life Church website (www.ulc.org), my status as Reverend was granted free, and entitles me to marry people and absolve them of sin -- though probably not in that order. For $5 extra, I can receive an official certificate proclaiming me to be anything from "Father" to "Universal Philosopher of Absolute Reality." For any doubting Thomases, don't worry -- they are supposed to send me a wallet card to confirm my legal status.

The ULC makes ends meet by selling ordinations over the Internet, as well as something called a "Ministry In A Box." Though the "church" seems torn from the pages of "Tax Dodging: 101," it reflects a growing trend among the theological community -- making productive use of the Internet. Evidently, the jokes I made in college about hoping to be the world's first "silicon chip" monk have been outdated by a Benedictine monk in Petersham, Massachusetts. Brother John Raymond rises each day in pre-dawn darkness to prepare for vigils, reading and meditation. Then he logs onto his computer.

More than ten years ago, Brother John took on what initially seemed a mundane chore at the rural monastery: maintaining the mailing list. Since then, it has grown by leaps and bounds. For hours at a time, he now answers prayer requests, reviews religious texts and updates an Internet site (www.monksofadoration.org) that broadcasts a live picture of the monastery's chapel around the clock.

The presence of religion on the Internet is nothing new. Even the Vatican has a website. However, the fusion of technology and spirituality is revolutionizing access to religious pursuits and theological discussions. Moreover, the Internet has the ability to spread the Gospel faster than ever before.

According to a recent report by the Washington Post, scores of monasteries in the United States now use the Internet. Dominican sisters in Michigan invite prayer requests for their "WebNun." Tibetan monks in New York offer online Buddhist studies and a blessing for cyberspace, and low chimes sound on the site of Coptic Orthodox monks in the California desert who are printers. Trappist monks in Kentucky pitch their abbey's 150th anniversary book after being inundated with orders for fruitcakes, cheese and bourbon fudge. A Benedictine monastery in California solicits donations for its "Adopt-a-Monk" program, while another in New Mexico is producing an interactive online liturgy in collaboration with IBM.

If only the Gideons could get with the program and put website addresses in hotel nightstands instead of Bibles, countless trees might be saved. One downside to reduced deforestation is that, if global climate changes stop, Vice President Gore would have little to talk about on the campaign trail. That Gore, who insists he is the "Father of the Internet," could be bested by "his" creation is not only ironic -- it's Oedipal. In a manner of speaking, I too will be a "Father" of the Internet. Once my $5 certificate arrives.

All things considered, Gore should think about getting ordained like me. Because it's nearly free, it won't cost him an arm, a leg or even a night's stay in the Lincoln Bedroom. In his bid for the White House, Gore's ability to absolve sins in exchange for votes would be a powerful campaign tool. Of course, getting votes from the President and First Lady might take up most of the campaign season.

On second thought, Gore should stick to the Internet and global warming and leave the business of forgiveness to the American people. And ministers like me.

An Impolite Jester

"Satire is a playfully critical distortion of the familiar."

-- Leonard Feinberg, American author

Felines, nothing more than felines...

Cats have taken a beating lately -- though not literally, I'm sorry to say. It's a metaphorical reference to the clobbering cats seem to be getting in some suburban areas -- not only for their predatory nature but also because of a campy Broadway musical. This is an expected consequence of cats not sticking up for themselves.

Felines, even those named "Snowball," have always been primal. For centuries, they relied on instinct to prowl around the home, using their natural predatory skills to hunt -- generally for furniture on which to urinate. Other than their own physical cravings, cats respond only to the Invisible Things Outside The Window That Only Cats Can See.

Most of what I know about cats came from Eartha Kitt in the 1960s on "Batman." Adam West seemed to have the same problems I do with cats -- chiefly, that they aren't very cooperative, they can turn on you in an instant, and they are usually involved with a plot to kidnap world leaders. And, it goes without saying that the puns cats use are purr-fectly cat-astrophic.

Some county governments, like Montgomery County, Maryland, have considered imposing cat leash laws. Many cat owners think this is cruel and unusual punishment -- they don't want to be tied to their cats, either. Cats are wild, untamed beasts who have survived unchanged throughout the ages, unpolished by the waters of evolution. This also seems to be the view of the National Geographic Society, who angered cat fans like Louise Holton for painting "an inaccurate, incomplete and sensational portrait of cats as murderous and sadistic, responsible for the wanton destruction of many native forms of wildlife."

Holton, president of Alley Cat Allies, a nationwide nonprofit organization, took steps to prevent distribution of "The Secret Life of Cats," a televised segment of the society's Explorer series, and continues to call on cat lovers to cancel their memberships with National Geographic. Holton warned that distribution of the documentary will encourage the needless killing of cats by making them "environmental scapegoats." Further, she requests "a more accurate documentary about feral cats and their behavior," especially concerning predation. In response, the National Geographic Society is said to be planning a four-part series focusing on "The Joy of Johnny Cat" and "World's Funniest Hairballs."

> "If we can de-claw cats, why can't we de-bone them?"

Unlike Holton, I dislike cats with an intensity that rivals the blinding heat of a thousand suns. Doesn't everybody? At a recent party, I asked "If we can de-claw cats, why can't we de-bone them?" Apparently, some members of People for the Ethical Treatment of Animals overheard me. As an animal myself, I found being tackled by animal rights fans more ironic than ethical. Luckily, they were vegetarians. They had a hard time writing "fur is murder" on me in carrot juice -- but not for lack of trying.

For the sake of argument, we should consider the value of selling cats to science. Cosmetic firms will pay top dollar for them, a point that I constantly share with homeless people looking to make a buck. Then, I give them the addresses of families with cats and let them have at it. Not only am I reducing the stray pet population, I am also creating jobs and empowering the less fortunate. One might say I'm killing three birds with one vagrant.

Cat lovers surely will agree with me that giving cats jobs in cosmetic labs is a good thing. Without jobs, cats slink around the house all day doing nothing other than sleeping, cleaning themselves and staring at Those Invisible Things -- sort of like I did the day after I graduated from high school.

Cosmetic testing labs give cats purpose, a raison d'etre. Moreover, if Charles Darwin's theory of evolution is correct, subjecting cats to the rigors of scientific testing will actually strengthen the feline race. By weeding out the weak, we are helping to create the Cat of Tomorrow -- a purposeful cat who looks good in hypoallergenic eyeliner. Imagine the sidewalks of your town, alive with cat-owners walking side-by-side with their well-groomed, well-coiffed cats at the end of a leash. Of course, the leashes wouldn't even be needed if Americans would reconsider the value of de-boning cats. It would be a new Golden Age.

The road to Hell may be paved with good intentions, but the road to Heaven is paved with dead cats.

Americans Are Dying to Litter

*V*arious methods of committing our physical form back to the Earth have been devised over the years. However, judging from the senseless polluting they do, dead people are dying to litter.

Case in point: in early November 1998, the body of John Konicek, buried at sea the year before, washed ashore near St. Augustine, Florida. This is the fourth body buried at sea that washed ashore or was found in Florida waters in recent years. Federal regulations require burials at sea be no closer than three miles with the body submerged to a depth of at least 100 fathoms, or about 600 feet. According to the Associated Press, Konicek most likely was dislodged from his casket by a passing hurricane. Whatever the case, it must be seen for what it is: post-mortem littering.

Cremation, the more common alternative to burial, gives family members the option to cast their dearly-departed to the wind -- literally. Scattering cremains from an airplane over a range of majestic mountains is very popular. However, thanks to the miracle of wind, few -- if any -- of the ashes actually land where intended. It is no mean feat explaining to grief-stricken family members that Uncle Harry landed in Nebraska instead of Nevada as they had hoped. Unless Uncle Harry's last wish was to ruin a picnic in Nebraska, in which case the wake would be alive with the sound of high-fives.

Scattering ashes by plane to memorialize those who are "gone with the wind" has come under fire -- largely by folks, like the disgruntled Nebraska picnickers, who tire of barbecued food peppered with cremains. Such concerns are easy fodder for the increasingly vocal anti-ash dumping movement. Some communities, chiefly resort towns, are horrified that ashes are being scattered in the waters near resort beaches. Rather than sinking, the ashes often end up on, or blow into, the faces of unsuspecting swimmers or sunbathers. Folks trying to enjoy the beaches of Massachusetts' Gay Head or Martha's Vineyard can expect to see their loved ones again soon -- in their swimming trunks and on their beach towels.

> "Most states places restrictions on the effluvient and related pollutants expelled into the air from crematories, yet any Tom, Dick, or Harry can take their relatives' ashes and dump them in a lake."

Ashes aside, there may also be health risks associated with crematories. A report by British medical researchers, which appeared in The Lancet,[5] indicates crematorium administrators and retort operators face elevated risks of mercury poisoning in the workplace, where countless dental fillings go up in smoke and mercury vapor. Ironically, there are more regulations placed on crematories' exhaust than on the ashes themselves. Most states place restrictions on the effluvient and related pollutants expelled into the air from crematories, yet any Tom, Dick, or Harry can take their relatives' ashes and dump them in a lake. As cemeteries become increasingly populated, and cremation continues to be a popular alternative, the blizzards of cremains becomes a serious pollution issue.

For families who bury their ashes rather than scattering them to the winds, thank you. America's outdoors enthusiasts appreciate it and believe ashflingers should try something else. In what might be called the "highway to heaven" method, cremains of the dearly-departed could supplement state highway departments' supplies of wintertime road sand. This way, even in death, people could save lives -- maybe even their own family's -- during treacherous wintertime driving.

Organ donation should not be the only post-mortem means of helping others. Until the dead start living up to their worldly responsibilities, Americans will keep making ashes of themselves for no good reason.

---

[5] November 14, 1998, to be exact.

Booming Future for Air Bags Predicted

*D*river-side air bags have created no shortage of controversy in the past few years. Traffic safety groups, like Public Citizen and Parents for Safer Air Bags, continue to pressure the National Highway Traffic Safety Administration (NHTSA) about its method of reviewing testing protocols of the devices. Such groups argue that air bags actually endanger lives by exploding outward with lethal force. Children and undersized adults seem to be at a higher risk of injury from the impact of the rapidly-inflating air bags. No one understands this better than automotive superpower DaimlerChrysler AG, who lost a $750,000 lawsuit in November 1998 to the father of a 5-year-old boy killed in an air bag-related injury.

In December 1998, the Associated Press reported the NHTSA's estimate that air bags have saved 3,600 lives and caused 121 deaths. With odds of nearly one in thirty that you will be killed in your next auto accident by one, comparing air bags to Russian roulette is not much of a stretch. Though they tend to prevent more injuries than they cause, with social problems like "tailgating," "drive-by shootings" and "road rage," experts should anticipate a booming air bag industry ahead.

Air bags have gotten a bad rap for their forthright way of greeting the chests of crash victims. Manufacturers of the devices seem stuck on the concept of "no pain, no gain." Frankly, the same technology which created air bags should be able to take the wind out of their impact. As the military uses "reactive armor" to protect certain vehicles against armor-piercing rounds, so too might drivers wear "airvests" that explode out toward the vehicle's primary air bag. The forces of each would counteract the other, resulting in a kinder, gentler car crash.

There is a risk, of course, that auto accidents would become so pleasant that folks might purposely collide with each other just for the pillowy sensation of safety.

Currently, air bags are gray and printed with the message "If you can read this, you're too close." In luxury models, the bags are made of leather and the message is handprinted in calligraphy. The forward-thinking lawyer will give up chasing ambulances in favor of advertising on air bags. Also, as consumer tastes develop, further variation among air bags is inevitable. Levi Strauss never imagined the day jeans would be made by artsy fashion houses like Jordache -- making designer air bags more probable than not.

For those who believe life is too short to take seriously, how about a driver-side whoopie cushion? The low note of a whoopie cushion would be a great commentary on life and to, as underscored by the old vaudeville axiom, "leave 'em laughing." Testing them in tiny clown cars, crammed with dozens of crash-test dummies in floppy shoes, seems appropriate.

> "Though inflatable dolls should be available in both genders to meet the tastes of the driver, an inflatable version of Edvard Munch's 'The Scream' might be the best choice."

For those who fear dying alone, a driver-side inflatable doll is a distinct possibility. Though inflatable dolls should be available in both genders to meet the tastes of the driver, an inflatable version of Edvard Munch's "The Scream" might be the best choice. Thanks to the miracle of technology, religious preferences could also be satisfied. For example, a driver-side inflatable priest could billow outward to comfort Catholic drivers in a crash. Not only would he cushion the blow, he could -- with help from a computerized sound chip -- give the pre-recorded last rites. A more secular use of sound chips might be to record the last wills and testaments of crash victims. Scoff if you must, but the day of driver-side "heir" bags may soon be at hand.

Mark my words, air bags will prove to be one of the most booming markets of the early 21st century. I, for one, plan to do everything possible to help my investments in the air bag industry grow. So, if you see me driving, get out of my way. With air bag investors like me on the road, "stock market crash" will take on a whole new meaning.

Fashion By NAFTA Is What We're AFTA

*N*ext to the last day before summer vacation, the first day of school was always my favorite. The buses smelled newer, and old friends *looked* newer -- some had new haircuts while others had tans. Most were a little taller than they'd been only three months before but one thing stood out above the rest: "back-to-school" clothes. After all, if one is returning to school another year older, one wants to look more sophisticated and worldly-wise.

This mentality never disappears, by the way. It returns at high-school class reunions, only more pronounced. Which reminds me -- I still need to return that solid gold tuxedo. Contrary to what I told my classmates, it was a rental. My point is, public schools are as much a fashion show now as they were in years past.

With increasingly crowded hallways, densely-packed classrooms and videogame-shortened tempers, schools are a haven for what sociologists are calling "hall rage." This is the indoor version of what sociologists have been calling "road rage," referring to the phenomenon of short-tempered drivers occasionally causing traffic accidents. Of course, hall rage is not new. In my day, we would frequently trip fellow students who were walking too slowly in front of us. Another means of hallway intimidation was accidentally stepping on the back of fellow students' shoes, causing what experts call a "flat tire." Such innocent hi-jinks these days likely would bring instant gunplay.

That said, modern students have options their forebears never did. Thanks to the North American Free Trade Agreement (NAFTA), it is now possible for students to bridge the gap between fashion and personal security. For example, the projectile-rich atmosphere of Bogota, Colombia, has led to an entire industry of bulletproof fashion. According to the Washington Post,[6] Caballero and Murphy Ltd., a Bogota firm selling custom-made bulletproof clothing, has seen sales rise 300 percent each year. The clothing is

---

[6] 1998.

available in varying degrees of ballistic resistance. For around $500, one can buy Level 1 gear to deflect small-caliber gunfire. Protection from 9mm Uzi submachine guns or other Level 4 gunfire can be had for about $800.

Protective dresswear comes in various colors, sizes and brand-names. In most cases, security experts line off-the-rack clothes, such as Tommy Hilfiger or Nautica, with sheets of lightweight bulletproof materials, like Kevlar, Spectra or Twaron. Security experts say that political candidates have been snapping up large quantities of fashionable bulletproof clothing -- from double-breasted sport coats and suits, to leather jackets and overcoats. In Colombia, such clothing is a needed supplement to the bulletproof podiums and armored cars used on the campaign trail.

> "In case the 'gun-free zones' surrounding America's school falter, it is nice to know that Kevlar-lined lunch boxes or backpacks are not far off."

Some firms have even started children's lines of bulletproof clothing. In case the "gun-free zones" surrounding America's schools falter, it is nice to know that Kevlar-lined lunch boxes or backpacks are not far off. However, be aware that some backpacks can kill you. The Consumer Product Safety Commission (CPSC) announced[7] that consumers should beware of "Mulan" backpacks, made by Pyramid Accessories Inc. Nearly 3,700 of the backpacks were recalled as its artwork contains lead, which medical experts remind us -- as would the ancient Greeks who used it for plumbing -- is toxic when ingested. One has to wonder about the quality of school lunches if children prefer chewing on lead-painted backpacks. At least they aren't going hungry.

This school year, special thanks should be given to NAFTA for helping the personal security of students remain fashionable. Hopefully, our North American trading partners will continue to help improve the American public education system -- perhaps by putting seatbelts in school buses. For now, perhaps we should be

---

[7] August 18, 1998, to be precise.

content that American kids are safer and more fashionable than ever before -- thanks to NAFTA and imported bulletproof clothing.

July 4th -- Dependence Day

*I*ndependence Day is one of America's favorite holidays. Some like the historic value of the day while others, like me, enjoy the arson and property damage encouraged on July 4th. Unfortunately, thanks to concerned parent groups and other safety-conscious wet blankets, it is increasingly difficult to celebrate Independence Day properly.

In the old days, we would save our money solely to buy as many firecrackers and bottle rockets as we could carry. No store needed shopping carts more than the friendly neighborhood fireworks store. My dad would drive us to the middle of nowhere to a Stuckey's, where a clapboard armory of Whistling Jupiters, smoke bombs and M-80s, held together by Black Cat posters, awaited young patriots and arsonists alike. My brother and I would also load up on Barbie dolls -- for the sheer pleasure of tying tiny explosives to them and setting them off. As one might imagine, Barbie had little staying power.

It wasn't long before we graduated to 14-inch Star Wars action figures that had greater durability. My brother would lay awake at night, dreaming of one day having enough money to buy a mannequin. I, on the other hand, would lay awake wondering how he could be laying awake dreaming. A mannequin was needed because our parents got mad when we tied firecrackers to the family dog. It is said there are no atheists in a foxhole. Likewise, on July 4th, every boy is either an arsonist or a sadist. We were a happy combination of both.

This was one of my main reasons for wanting a drivers' license. I needed the freedom to drive to Stuckey's for more weaponry and ordnance whenever I wanted. Thankfully, after two tries, I passed my driving test and immediately drove to the city limits to stock up. That it was October didn't seem to matter. Patriots like me believe every day is Independence Day and, even in the dead of winter, I planned to celebrate accordingly. A Chewbacca doll I'd gotten for my birthday had been talking up socialism. Until I straightened him

73

out, a 14-inch revolution was blowing in the wind. It would have been like "Toy Story" written by Bolsheviks. Fortunately, I got there in time and, with the help of four Roman candles, made short work of that uprising.

> "July 4th has become less a celebration of independence than one of oppression disguised as 'public safety.'"

Unfortunately, there are plenty of laws preventing my special blend of patriotism and property damage. Sparklers, a perennial favorite, are now condemned as dangerous around dry weeds. Similarly, bottle rockets are frowned upon because they could fly out of control and hurt somebody. These days, you can't even put loads of diesel and fertilizer in your rented Ryder truck without people getting bent out of shape. As a result, July 4th has become less a celebration of independence than one of oppression disguised as "public safety."

Such public safety laws are driving fireworks stands out of business, leaving fewer each year to meet the patriotic needs of Americans. It is not hard to imagine a day when all fireworks are outlawed. Unfortunately, this will leave Americans with only one way to celebrate their freedom from the British -- shooting guns in the air and setting cars on fire.

Fireworks must be illegal in Europe. It is the only explanation for post-game fights between European police and crazed soccer fans drunk on Molotov cocktails. Without firecrackers, one's natural destructive energies can be released only through blinding public violence. The controversial "Ultimate Fighting Championship" may have gotten started this way in a town that illegalized fireworks. Conversely, Disneyland and Walt Disney World both do giant fireworks displays each night and report surprisingly few riots or public disturbances. It all adds up.

If they want to make communities safer, parents and public leaders should reconsider their stance on fireworks. Also, I would appreciate any information on how my brother can get a mannequin with no questions asked.

Be Different... Just Like Me

*A*mericans have been infected by an intense love for the 1970s, a disease I call "Spyro Gyral Meningitis." From bell-bottomed slacks to Volkswagen Bugs, the nation has been contaminated with the Polyester Decade. Where is the Surgeon General with a quarantine when you really need one?

The Fox network, who is to bad television as Mary was to typhoid, is exacerbating this plague with 1970s-themed programs like "That '70s Show." Fox hopes "That '70s Show" will survive America's cultural short-term attention span. With your help, we can ensure that it doesn't. When it appears on my television, I immediately turn to another channel and I encourage you to do the same. If you haven't seen this mind-numbing send-up of the Butterfly Collar Era, consider yourself lucky.

Surely I'm not the only American fed up with the 1970s. I hope I'm not. Everywhere I go, young people are rejoicing in 1970s kitsch. Hip-hugger pants, platform shoes, straight hair and muttonchop sideburns are as plentiful as White House legal defense strategies. No one seems to understand that the 1970s is a decade best left behind. It is said that if you can remember the 1960s, you weren't really there. I believe that if you can remember the 1970s, you're not really trying.

For those who are too young to remember this blight on America's past, let me fill you in. The 1970s was a decade, approximately ten years in duration, that featured the rise of corduroy and the fall of khaki. Navels were in, as was body-painting and sandals with a special strap of leather to keep the big toe from getting away. It was a completely different world.

Orange Crush and Nehru jackets were big, until the Beatles broke up -- paving the way for the Pepsi Generation and Neil Diamond's era of "Forever in Blue Jeans." Discotheques were as numerous as Starbuck's Coffee bars. Cell phones were the big black rotaries used by inmates and people thought "Power Rangers" were burly forest officials.

Saturday Night Live was still in its infancy and featured a dark-tressed piano player named Paul Schaffer. Adrian had yet to tell Rocky he couldn't win, and roller boogie was the order of the day. The "Mach I" was the coolest car on the road, though no one ever saw dealerships for them. Perhaps they were sold through the mail from ads in the back of comic books -- the same place one could buy Sea Monkeys and enlist to deliver Grit newspapers. No one ever saw Grit newspapers either but, if one sold enough of them, one could earn a "mini-bike." The mini-bike was essentially a tiny motorcycle with fat knobby tires, like a cross between a motorcycle, a monster truck and a dwarf. Motorcycles were big in the 1970s, and the most popular man alive was patriotic stuntman Evel Knievel.

> "[In the 1970s] people thought 'Power Rangers' were burly forest officials."

America was in love with stuntmen. We even had a stuntman in the White House: President Gerald Ford. Each week on "Saturday Night Live," President Ford would do a different stunt -- sometimes tripping down the steps of Marine One and other times crashing through his desk in the Oval Office. Of course, in 1977, he was defeated by the disco president -- Jimmy Carter, the first Chief Executive to use a blowdryer. From Carter's brother, Billy, to sightings of "killer rabbits" and UFOs in the Nation's capital, the Carter administration is best memorialized in the television sitcom, "Carter Country." Such memorable television shows almost made inflation, gas shortages, and "Charlie's Angels" tolerable.

Who is to blame for this explosion of 1970s mania? Former video store employee Quentin Tarantino, and no one else. If not for his blood-spattered movie "Pulp Fiction," which glamorized such things as sideburns, afros and the "Bat-Dance," we would be reminiscing about the 1980s right now -- like the nation did one weekend in 1998.

That the 1980s didn't catch on then was no surprise. After all, the 1980s was about rebellion. We didn't like trends or fads back then, and we still don't. Because of the 1980s, modern America is bent on non-conformity. It's important to be different just like everybody else. With that in mind, be different like me and join the fight against the 1970s and the spread of Spyro Gyral Meningitis.

Being a Juror Is Civic Doody

I emerged from the flame of civic duty unharmed, but not unchanged. You see, I recently was drafted for jury duty. At first, it seemed like a great opportunity to be a part of the judicial process and exercise my right as a citizen. However, I quickly learned that the judicial process is a big machine in which the juror is a tiny cog. Upon arriving, juror candidates stand in a line to get a card that is pinned or likewise affixed to them so they won't forget who they are. According to mine, I was "Petit Juror No. 141." That's sort of long and stand-offish so I started asking people to call me "PJ-141" for short. It seemed friendlier.

Soon thereafter, all the PJs were herded into a large pen named "The Lounge." Something of a misnomer, I should say, because no one was lounging. By my count, there were exactly one bazillion people crammed into too few seats, holding their ears in defiance of the two television sets blaring loudly from a bolted perch 20 feet above us. Similarly, The Lounge's chairs were bolted to the floor making it impossible to turn the sound down without it turning into some sort of circus routine. The best we could manage was to whack feebly at the TVs with a broomstick somebody found in a janitor's closet. It was like a pinata only with no blindfolds, no candy and, other than accidentally increasing the volume, no apparent effect.

Hour after hour, Vicki Lawrence and the interminably-lackwitted "Mama's Family" attempted to entertain us at decibel-levels normally reserved for leaf blowers. This may have been the court's attempt to induce mind-control, like the Soviets did in the Cold War. Those Soviets may not have known much about economics, but they sure knew their auditory punishments. Thanks in part to "Mama's Family," I soon was surrounded by a roomful of zombies carrying cards like mine. We surely would have blacked out from sensory overload if not for a loud, unintelligible voice crackling through the loudspeaker announcing the numbers of juror candidates called to the courtroom. Unfortunately my number was not called, so I rejoined the battle with Vicki Lawrence and her horde of laughtrack-supported japesters -- Attila the Pun, in a manner of speaking.

Half an hour later, the loudspeaker shook us out of our mindless reverie and called my number, and those of 23 others, instructing us to wait in yet another line. With zombie-like plod, we shuffled out of The Lounge. Once our group was deemed worthy, we entered the courtroom where we were sworn in and had to answer provocative questions like "Has anyone here a medical ailment or condition that would prevent them from participating fully in this trial?" It was amazing how few arms were raised at that one. After the mindbending treatment we'd had in The Lounge, I was half-tempted to yell out "Vertigo!" and call it a day. But I hung in there as did my 23 cohorts.

> "It must have been either my boyish good looks or my 'I'm With Guilty' t-shirt featuring an arrow pointing at the defendant."

Nearly twenty minutes passed until the lawyers were allowed to weed out those they felt would not render their desired verdict. It wasn't long before I was selected out. In retrospect, it must have been either my boyish good looks or my "I'm With Guilty" t-shirt featuring an arrow pointing at the defendant. Whatever the case, I was bounced and sent back to The Lounge for more mind-control.

There were still nearly one bazillion PJs who'd been there from before, all staring tearfully into the televisions high above them. Happily, "Mama's Family" was no longer being shown. Instead, it was that movie from the 1970s. You know the one -- it had dim lighting, vinyl-looking leather jackets, a lot of whispering and screaming. They were probably screaming because they had to wear those lousy vinyl-looking leather jackets. Worse, the jackets were cut like sportcoats.

An entire afternoon of that movie packed wall-to-wall with bad fashion -- topped with bad loudspeakers -- accounts for the king-sized headache I kept as a souvenir from my day in court. Many of us were not called again so, after what seemed an eternity, we were allowed to escape. I now have some understanding of what

Eisenhower saw in 1944 when he inspected Nazi concentration camps. The PJs who had to stay behind looked at us with big, sad eyes that seemed to plead "Tell others what happened here." Those poor, wretched souls reminded me of Dustin Hoffman in "Papillon."

Headaches won out over sympathy, so my fellow jury parolees and I formed one last line -- a line to turn in our PJ nametags and to collect a handsome fee of $2 for our trouble. That's right -- two measly dollars, which I plan to contribute to the Juror Victimization Fund, if there is one. With enough contributions, the fund could buy a crowbar with which to pry those televisions off the ceiling and bash the screens in.

Yes, I emerged unharmed but not unchanged. Who says jury duty doesn't give you a better sense of civic responsibility?

The Evils of Public Grooming

*I*t happened again today. Over the din of workaday life, I heard it. TIK -- the sound of someone thoughtlessly clipping their fingernails in the office. To the untrained ear, the sound is easily mistaken for the sound of a pen being clicked into action. However, to me, it is a call to arms not unlike Batman's "bat signal." Greater attention must be paid to this growing social evil. Unfortunately, the Occupational Safety and Health Administration (OSHA) is either unable or unwilling to address this political hot potato. For this reason, cracking down on the menace of officewide fingernail clipping is my lonely responsibility.

For letting something like this get to me, psychologists likely will contend that I am obsessive-compulsive because of unresolved issues from my childhood. Some of you will snicker and make fun of me for what seems a ridiculous pet peeve. Fine. We'll see how funny you think it is when a piece of clipped fingernail buries itself in your eye.

Some will argue that there are other, more unsafe, practices in need of public attention, from sneezing into one's hands before using one's computer keyboard or mouse, to having a piece of gunk in their eye from what some say is from "Mr. Sandman." However, even in a public area, people usually have the grace to turn away while tidying up their schmutz-covered tear duct. Though it is tough to support "personal displays of grooming" (PDOG) like schmutz removal, it pales in comparison to public fingernail clipping. There is little chance of injuring bystanders from secondhand eyegunk. Underscoring this, a wise man once observed, "The only thing worse than finding a fingernail clipping in your potato salad is *not* finding it."

The habit of public grooming is not only distasteful, it is a slippery slope. If allowed to persist, employers may have to issue batting helmets and goggles to protect workers from the blizzards of flying fingernails. What is the alternative? Scarred eyeballs and facial lacerations can make employees surprisingly litigious. Worse, it may lead to such things as flossing during business meetings, cleaning out one's toenails in church and even Q-tipping one's ears clean in restaurants. Experts worry that workplace PDOGs may eventually lead to worldwide hygiene problems and reductions in global human wellness. Sadly, it may not be possible to put the PDOG genie back in its bottle.

What then is the solution to the spectre of increased PDOG activities? There are three options, besides physically accosting public groomers: First, ridicule them publicly. Tarring and feathering is a good start. Second, encourage your elected officials to create stiffer sentences for PDOG crimes. Write them as often as possible, decrying public grooming and pleading for stricter regulations on fingernail-clipping in the workplace.

> "If search and seizure worked with spinning wheels back in the days of Sleeping Beauty, it surely would work with modern-day fingernail clippers."

Third, encourage city and county officials to illegalize fingernail clipper use. Zoning ordinances should be amended to include limits on workplace grooming for reasons of public safety. Law enforcement officials could seize and impound fingernail clippers in their jurisdictions, like they do with guns of felons and gang members. It would be a costly effort, sure, but not as costly as an unsafe workplace. If search and seizure worked with spinning wheels back in the days of Sleeping Beauty, it surely would work with modern-day fingernail clippers. With your help, we can end the menace of the public grooming and make our workplaces safe again.

TIK. There's that sound again -- who is doing that?

Rolling Stones Should Gather No Mas

*I*f you're like me, you are more than ready for spring. Winters are difficult each year, from the troublesome get-togethers with families you tolerate less and less, to crummy gifts that either don't fit or are too tacky to wear. Then there's Valentine's Day, when one goes out of one's way to get jewelry or a box of candy for one's sweetheart only, in turn, to be told "Doug, I'm seeing someone else." Strangely, one never gets those gifts back. The romantic holiday last year was complicated further by the need to put my dog to sleep. It was especially tough because he was an insomniac.

To cheer myself up, I spent $300 to go see the Rolling Stones in concert. It was their last tour, gerontologists predicted, so I went for the historical value if nothing else. I sneaked backstage and was amazed at all the drugs those guys do -- Zantac, One-A-Day, Senokot... lots of Senokot. Apparently, Mick hasn't been prancing about on stage all these years. He's just never had a vegetable-based laxative like Senokot.

Given the Rolling Stones' advanced age and obvious lack of Depends undergarments, crowd members near the stage were warned, "The first four rows *WILL* get wet." It was sort of like a "Gallagher" comedy show only with more hair and less bowel control. Their song "Brown Sugar" seemed a little ironic, and more than a little interactive. No wonder the crowd complained of having "crappy" seats!

The show was pretty typical, I suppose, though I am hardly a Rolling Stones fan. I recognized "Jumping Jack Flash" as the theme from a less-than-stellar Whoopi Goldberg movie of the same name, and "Start Me Up" as the campaign theme song for Sen. Strom Thurmond (R-S.C.). However, most of the other songs were only vaguely familiar. It must be said that the only thing worse than the Rolling Stones' *new* songs was the sight of female AARP members flashing Mick. With all their sagging, drooping and swinging, I was surprised Mick didn't launch into "Gimme Shelter." Those flailing tentacles reminded me of Doctor Octopus from Marvel Comics. If

I hadn't been taught to duck-and-cover in grade school nuclear assault drills, I could have been injured. Because some of those topless Gray Panthers might actually have been grade school teachers once, Show and Tell will never be the same for me again. It was telling, indeed, to see Mick roaming about a stage littered with support hose.

> "It was telling, indeed, to see Mick roaming about a stage littered with support hose."

One has to wonder about the Rolling Stones. They sold out long ago. Once they were the "bad boys" of rock and roll, but now they rely on sponsorships from button-down corporations. In select cities, McDonald's is trying to promote the Rolling Stones tour with a limited edition Rolling Stones sandwich that they call the "McJagger." Having tried one, I honestly think the McJagger is made mostly out of lips. I say that because mine had a cold sore and the less said about the special sauce the better. That said, the McJagger is a step up from the "McBeal" which is just skin and bones on two small buns.

Needless to say, the concert did little to lighten my mood. I remain bitter and loveless, and $300 poorer than I was. I apologize to those who hoped I would conclude with an uplifting message of inspiration and hope. It's just not there. Considering my dog, my love life and all the aged exhibitionists at the concert, I am simply too depressed to be much good to anyone. Maybe things will be better in the spring.

Improving the Complexion of the Modern Workplace

*M*y last girlfriend wasn't Italian but her face was somewhat Ziti. Given that experience, I consider myself learned on the effects bad complexions can have on others. While there are many medical reasons for the bad acne suffered by some, most folks with bad complexions have only themselves to blame. Teenagers are the obvious target of this little diatribe but I have a more specific one in mind: a guy in my office.

This man's complexion is largely clear, with the exception of a large mound on his cheek. It looks like a fleshy marble, except that it has hair growing out of it -- even in the cleavage next to his cheek -- suggesting it may actually be some sort of large polyp or mole. He probably has to shave it with clippers. I don't know for sure and I don't care, really. I just want it away from me.

Grueling is the only way to describe having to sit through meeting after meeting with that dermatological horror leering at my cheek like it's a piece of meat, which it is, or choice real estate. The only thing I want hanging from my cheek is a cute girl, and I'm not picky about which one.

The assumption that my colleague's "cheekbutton" is a blemish may be utterly wrong. Rather, it may be a form of facial insurance -- like a bumper, or a tiny driver-side airbag one can take along wherever one goes. Why should drivers have all the protection? There are *plenty* of workaday collisions to merit having an airbag affixed to one's cheek.

Another possibility is that it is a stress-reliever, like those desk novelties sold in the Lillian Vernon catalog. A quick squeeze of his subcutaneous stress-reliever could be just what my co-worker needs to stay calm during tense moments. Of course, someone needing a stress-reliever so often that surgical implantation is an option is probably too volatile to be effective in the workplace anyway.

Maybe the reason I steal glances at his faceberg is because it looks so… breastlike. Renowned psychiatrist Dr. Sigmund Freud would probably agree but "mama's boys" like him usually have one-track minds anyway. Freud surely would postulate that the reason people, when in private, can't stop fidgeting with their pimples is that, on some level, humans are naturally attracted to breasts. Pimples are not unlike breasts. After all, displaying them publicly is considered shameful, and both should be fondled only in private.

Freud would have us believe that, on some level, humans crave the maternal protection and nurturing of which the breast is a conspicuous symbol. The role of the mother in modern complexion control cannot be understated. Many is the mother who asks "Why don't you do something about that pimple?"

> "Because of all the ski masks they wear, bank robbers probably don't concern themselves much with the dermatology of their co-workers."

If it isn't a pimple, perhaps my co-worker's hairy little doorknob should be addressed as the small breast that it is. I should check with the Human Resources department to see if there is any way to require he cover it with a bra or some similar breast-concealing device. Tassles or even a Band-Aid would be a big improvement over this garish state of affairs. If large breasts can be reduced surgically, it follows that similar techniques might be used to correct facial imbalances like his. Because of all the ski masks they wear, bank robbers probably don't concern themselves much with the dermatology of their co-workers. Unfortunately, I am not in the bank robbery business.

That a subcutaneous golf ball has remained on my colleague's face for who-knows-how-long suggests that maybe he likes it. If so, his facial imbalance could be enhanced by implanting a *second* cheek polyp on the other side of his face. Sure, it sounds odd but at least they would match. Whatever the case, the little Jiffy Pop-shaped growth on the side of his face is distracting.

Former First Lady "Lady Bird" Johnson encouraged an entire nation to "Beautify America." With this in mind, consider cosmetic surgery to stunt those growths. It won't take long and it can't cost much. Until you get cosmetic surgery, your co-workers will continue to want to attack your face with a butter knife to improve your appearance. Afterwards, everyone will feel better, you will look better, and your work environment will improve.

This partly explains why my girlfriend broke up with me, and her sudden aversion to butter knives, but it was a small price to pay for improving our office's productivity.

Now, if you'll excuse me, I'm late for a staff meeting and I'm in charge of the butter knife.

The Life You Save May Lead to the Next Hitler

*W*hen interviewed about their longevity, many octogenarians report the secret to long life is not worrying about things. If there is any validity to such claims, I won't make it to 40. I worry about a lot. For example, after seeing the movie "Private Parts," I worried that Howard Stern might have been typecast. He may find it hard to break out of that stereotype. The same problem has limited the careers of Tina Louise, a.k.a. Ginger from "Gilligan's Island," Max Baer, a.k.a. Jethro from "The Beverly Hillbillies," and O.J. Simpson, a.k.a. Not Guilty from "CourtTV."

There are other examples which worry me. Recently, after hearing his choking and gagging, I applied the Heimlich maneuver to a co-worker. Life-saving techniques come naturally to me because, several years ago, I bought a Resusci-Annie for my own personal use. Not only does she help me practice CPR and other emergency treatments, she's cheaper than one of those "Real Sex" dolls. She's not much of a talker but, on the other hand, she is a good listener. That I don't have to pay for her when I take her to movies is icing on the cake, but I digress.

After my anaerobic colleague coughed up what appeared to be a chunk of sausage, onlookers commended me on my quick reaction to what may have been a life-threatening situation. In truth, I acted not out of valor but, instead, because his gagging was very loud. I went to his office not to give aid but to say "Shut up! I'm on the phone!" Cubicles don't give much privacy anyway, but his choking noises made it difficult for me to focus on my conversation with Bob in Accounting. This is one of the advantages of e-mail -- conversations through cyberspace aren't as likely to be interrupted by the obnoxious sounds of self-absorbed co-workers caught up in their own choking. "Save ME." "Help ME." It's always "Me, Me, Me" with some people.

Once we'd dislodged the sausage morsel from his gullet, my colleague was grateful for my saving his life. At least, that's what I make of his thank-you card. It features a dog, digging comically through a backyard near a big pile of bones. The inside reads "Thanks a heap" which, I figure, is a reference to the pile he hacked up on the floor. For saving one's life, a card is always a nice touch. However, I noticed it was not a Hallmark card suggesting he wasn't all that grateful. Worrying that he was just trying to kill himself and I scotched his plans is worrisome indeed.

I also worry that it may have been God's will that he choke to death that day. If it was, and I interfered, I'm screwed. God doesn't forget things like that. He's still sore about that stunt we pulled with the apple. Remember that? Christian Scientists do. What's more, they believe that, if you're choking, it is because God wants it that way. To them, if you die, that's God's way of teaching you an important "life lesson."

I also worry that my co-worker -- the man I saved -- may one day have a child that grows up to become the next Hitler. If so, my act of selfless heroism may well result in the death of millions. Because I don't know if I can live with that sort of guilt, I plan to buy my colleague a ham sandwich and hope nature takes its course. It worked for "Mama" Cass Elliott and it is sure to work for me. If nothing else, it will be one less thing for me to worry about.

News and Comment

"The human race was one really effective weapon, and that is laughter."

-- Mark Twain, American humorist

Insurance Industry Unveils Pet Project

*A*merica is traditionally a nation of dog lovers. How else could pet psychiatry have survived this long? While it has long been a staple of scam artists and comedians, pet psychiatry is giving way to a cottage industry of other pet services -- from medical insurance to estate planning. It may not be long before dogs are required to carry organ donor tags on their collars.

Veterinary Pet Insurance (VPI), based in California, has sold more than 750,000 pet policies since its founding 18 years ago. VPI President Jack Stevens recently told reporters that his firm expects to double its business this year, and expects the pet insurance trend to continue. "They're part of the family," Stevens said, "and people want to take care of them." According to the Associated Press, VPI currently covers 6,500 known medical conditions, exempting hereditary and congenital conditions.

VPI isn't alone. Rewards Plus of America (RPA), a Maryland-based business which puts together employee benefits packages for firms, added pet insurance to its litany of mutual fund and term-life insurance products. In the first six months it was offered, pet insurance became one of RPA's most popular voluntary benefits.

Why the need for pet insurance? Ask your local veterinarian. From gene therapy to the prosthetic sciences, medical technologies have advanced at all levels -- from the doctor's office to the veterinarian's stainless steel pet table. Specialty care for modern pets doesn't come cheap. Exotic treatment, like kidney transplants and chemotherapy, can cost thousands of dollars. In fact, according to some veterinary specialists, money may be the only limit on what services modern pets can receive.

Examples of veterinary advances include pet angioplasty -- also known as "balloon valvioplasty" -- and "limb sparring." The technique, pioneered by veterinary oncologists at Colorado State University, gives pets with cancer-ridden legs an option besides amputation. Though it costs about twice as much as amputation, limb sparring features the grafting of healthy, non-cancerous bones from animals that died of non-infectious diseases.

> "'Faux Paws' will not only help pet amputees lead an active lifestyle again, it also will make me rich."

Pets with more cost-conscious owners may be interested in my brand-new line of prosthetic limbs for pets. "Faux Paws" will not only help pet amputees lead an active lifestyle again, it also will make me rich. Stay tuned for my forthcoming home surgery kit, which I plan to call either "The Ace of Spayeds" or "Puppy Ciao."

Speaking of surgical innovations, veterinary surgeons at the University of California (Davis) School of Veterinary Medicine, currently perform between 25 and 40 kidney transplants each week on pets. John Wooldridge, a small-animal surgeon, told reporters the procedure works best on cats because they tend to accept new organs better than other animals. The procedure, which can cost as much as $4,000, is intended for cats that, renal disease aside, are otherwise healthy. While the costs of such pet-saving techniques are high, some will argue that no price is too high to keep pets around.

Pets are frequently considered part of the family, and are seen as especially valuable to senior citizens and those with certain disabilities. But what happens to King, Spot or Mittens when their owner dies? Supermarket tabloids routinely report on a dying millionaire leaving the family fortune to the family cat. Because pets aren't legally entitled to be beneficiaries of estates or trusts, even FDR knew the notion of an heir-dale terrier is a "Fala-cy." However, an increasing number of pet owners are starting pet trusts to ensure that, in the event of their death, the lifestyle of their pet is maintained.

Only in America would pets have it better than humans in third-world countries. Clearly, our country has gone to the dogs.

Historic Significance Takes a Holiday

*A*s many may recall, in 1996, Washington's National Airport was renamed by Congress to honor President Ronald Reagan. The so-called "Ronald Reagan National Airport" required a collossal amount of political maneuvering. Some obstacles included the beliefs of some that renaming anything for a living president is bad policy.

An airport is a fine way to honor someone but, in truth, the hope of all presidents is that succeeding generations will reward them with their own *holiday*. The standard is set by the birthdays of both George Washington and Abraham Lincoln, who remain the only U.S. presidents to have holidays named for them. That the two birthday celebrations are lumped together into one homogenous "President's Day" shows two things: America likes celebratory efficiency, and Americans dislike federal employees getting additional days off.

Holidays are not the only way to honor former presidents. Washington has an entire state named for him, not to mention the District of Columbia -- originally to have been named Washingtonopolis. The Father of Our Country has a national forest named for him, too, and a university, many counties, thousands of schools, city parks, streets and even a parkway in Virginia.

Not to be outdone, Lincoln has a city named for him as well as some counties, a national highway, a successful chain of technical schools, a tunnel in New York City, a style of debating and a popular line of log-based children's toys. Ironically, U.S. presidents often ride in bulletproof Lincolns.

Because no president has matched Washington or Lincoln in popularity, America's leaders are left with comparatively pitiful honors. Clearly, however, naming an airport after Reagan is consistent with our nation's trend of naming modes of transportation after our leaders.

Reagan joins John F. Kennedy in the airport category, while Lyndon Johnson has a space center named for him (which is really nothing more than a Texas-sized airport). Woodrow Wilson has a bridge named for him, and Gerald Ford joins Lincoln in the automotive department. Both Teddy and Franklin Roosevelt have ships named for them, while George Bush has both an expressway in Dallas and the headquarters of the Central Intelligence Agency in northern Virginia.

> "General Motors would do well to name a car after Harry Truman -- a good slogan might be 'The Buick stops here!'"

Unfortunately, not every president receives these sort of honors. Richard Nixon deserved, at least, to be the mascot of a tape recording company. General Motors would do well to name a car after Harry Truman -- a good slogan might be "The Buick stops here!"

Besides a nuclear submarine, the only thing named for Jimmy Carter was a lousy TV show in the early 1980s called "Carter Country." The show featured a redneck police department that made the Keystone Cops look like Scotland Yard. Perhaps the dimwittery and slack-jawed boobulence glorified each week was a metaphor for Carter's bungled mission to rescue American hostages in Iran. Whatever the case, it didn't take long before Carter Country was replaced with the far-superior "What A Country!" starring President Reagan's favorite Russian comedian, Yakov Smirnoff.

Generally, America enjoys honoring its presidents with airports, expressways, highways and tunnels. This speaks volumes about America's subconscious desire to see its leaders hit the road.

With this in mind, Republicans plan to name a getaway car for President Clinton, having bungled their opportunity in 1999 to give him a moving van. However, Republicans will celebrate the anniversary of Mr. Clinton moving out of the White House for years to come. This may be good news to the Man From Hope because having a national holiday named for you beats a renamed airport any day of the week.

FDA Reform Goes To Pot

As many Americans are aware, undue amounts of attention are growing thanks to the labors of the progressive medicine bandwagon. While the subject of the legalization of marijuana for medicinal purposes is rife with questions, I humbly offer these comments at the risk of undeservedly glamorizing a subject unworthy of public discussion – the taming of the "shroom," as it were.

Though Arizona passed a similar measure, the passage of California's "Proposition 215" in 1997 -- which legalized marijuana for general medical use through a very broad "any other illness" clause -- should face more scrutiny than it has.

Supporters argue any number of benefits to the use of cannibis, such as treatment of glaucoma, cancer, AIDS- or HIV-related symptoms. However, such specious claims have yet to be borne out by science. "Now that marijuana is legal," some might suggest, "maybe crack cocaine should be too. It could end world hunger since amphetamines reduce hunger pangs." This same thinking proposes to give Rohypnol[8] to AIDS victims so they will black out and forget that they're suffering.

Not surprisingly, there is very little data on how many cases of glaucoma or cancer have been cured by marijuana. A quick call to the FDA for assistance was fruitless. Their voicemail message said "Sorry we can't take your call right now, 'cuz we're all just BAKED, man! One love, and pass the dutchie on the left hand side (beeeeep)." I'm pretty sure I heard reggae music in the background.

With the passage of measures such as Prop. 215, and Arizona's Prop. 200, what sort of examples are being set for our children? "Honey, Mommy has a headache... could you bring me a doobie? It's in my purse, under the condoms and next to the hypodermic

---

[8] More commonly called "Roofie," rohypnol is a widely-used "date rape" drug.

needles." By endorsing marijuana use, these states have clearly chosen Janis Joplin over June Cleaver -- which is ironic because Mrs. Cleaver, a resident of the Golden State, continues to work in the entertainment industry. In contrast, Ms. Joplin only appears at the occasional seance and even then is surprisingly tight-lipped.

> "There is an increasingly fine line between health care and a Pink Floyd concert."

Thanks to Props. 215 and 200, there is an increasingly fine line between health care and a Pink Floyd concert. If pot is designated a medicine, what next? Will the FDA work to classify M&Ms as dietary supplements? Given time, they probably will. After all, there are some Americans who currently supplement their diets with M&Ms. Others subsist entirely on them. Rep. Jerrold Nadler (D-N.Y.) comes to mind, as does Karne Wilson of the singing trio Wilson Phillips. You may not remember Ms. Wilson because she cleverly wore baggy clothing and, like the wily chameleon, became virtually invisible against the background of her svelte singing partners.

Legalizing illegal recreational drugs, like marijuana, only hastens America's descent into the chasm of immorality. Thanks to the medical community's belief in preventive medicine, people will be able to exploit the "any other illness" clause to use marijuana to *minimize* their chances of getting glaucoma. On a positive note, legalized marijuana would surely improve America's snack consumption. Sales of brownies, Frito-Lay corn chips, and other fatty foods will skyrocket nearly as fast as America's collective cholesterol.

It is sad that the nation our patriot forefathers fought and died for will soon be overrun by a bunch of stoned-out junkies strung out on Little Debbie snack cakes. All in the name of "preventive medicine" and dubious medical reasoning.

Due to the current backlog of requests for FDA approval of various medical treatments, Congress is currently working to speed up the agency's approval process. With reviews of new cancer-fighting techniques, AIDS treatments, and new biomedical devices galore, the FDA has an unquestionably full plate.

Contrary to what proponents of legalized marijuana will tell you, the FDA doesn't need to waste its time and resources trying to get bong hits covered by Blue Cross. Kids need to learn that "drug-free" doesn't mean letting the insurance company pay for it.

Just Say No to Naval Helmets?

For generations, children have been told to beware of things that go bump in the night. Modern kids ought also to fear things that go bump underwater -- namely, two nuclear-powered submarines that collided during training maneuvers off New York's Long Island in early 1998. The Associated Press reported that the USS San Juan, a fast-attack sub and the USS Kentucky, a Trident, both returned to Groton, Connecticut, under their own power for extensive checks after the watery fender bender.

That there were no injuries nor any radioactive leakage is a miracle, considering our nuclear fleet -- or "nook-yuh-ler" fleet, as some elected officials call it -- is built by the lowest bidder. Thankfully, sometimes you get more than you pay for.

It didn't take long for the regulatory vultures to begin circling, hungry to enact numerous safety measures aimed at preventing similar maritime accidents from happening again. Their recommendations are likely to include a call for underwater speed limits, manufacturer-installed bumpers, a slew of seatbelt laws, kneepads and the mandatory use of helmets.

Helmet use has been a staple of the regulatory movement since the collision-related deaths of Michael Kennedy and Rep. Sonny Bono (R-Calif.). Sources say medical professionals support the voluntary use of helmets among sailors, as well as among jet-ski operators, lifeguards and cliff divers.

Unfortunately, helmets -- which sell for $30 to $160 -- provide only limited protection to submariners traveling at speeds of up to 45 knots surrounded by water pressures of thousands of pounds per square inch. Even 19th century futurist Jules Verne knew that helmets are of little use 20,000 leagues under the sea.

In addition, some believe helmet use will encourage people to abandon caution and behave recklessly underwater. At present, according to proponents of helmet use, there are no bodies of water specifically requiring helmet use. "We consider helmets a second line of defense," a spokesman said. In this case, the first line of defense is responsible submarining.

Historically, America's regulatory community has always drifted towards disaster. Regulators benefit from the momentum caused by national attention about such accidents, which propels forward the cause du jour. Lately, helmets are being touted as the answer to everything from skiing and rollerblading, to El Nino and campaign finance reform. Unfortunately, calls for helmets reflect the knee-jerk policymaking typical of Washington.

> "If trapped underwater in a submarine, 'diver-side air bags' are much more practical than helmets."

Helmets are not necessarily the appropriate response to tragedy -- at least, not in the area of submarine safety. When one considers the Pentagon's tradition of paying hundreds of dollars for toilet seats, what sort of expense would taxpayers incur if the Navy began using helmets? Frankly, if trapped underwater in a submarine, "diver-side air bags" are much more practical than helmets. Sailors would breathe easier if such common-sense safety precautions were available.

Another option is one that has spent far too long on the drawing board. Submarines, like the San Juan and Kentucky, all have torpedo tubes. It ought to be simplicity itself for submarine manufacturers to install torpedo-shaped escape pods. In times of crisis, a submarine crew could easily be torpedoed out through the tubes to safety on dry land. Sure, the landing may be a little uncomfortable but it has to be better than being trapped at the bottom of the ocean wearing a helmet. Even in 1912, the doomed passengers of the Titanic would have endorsed "emergency evacu-tubes." Probably.

Calls for maritime helmet use probably will not be considered by Congress this year, nor even next. Should regulators push the issue, conservatives in Congress, who hate an overly regulatory executive branch, are expected to oppose it. Until the issue can be decided by elected officials, a laissez-faire compromise may be simply to encourage submarines -- indeed, *ALL* submersible watercraft -- to affix bumperstickers reading "How's my diving? Call 1-800-USA-NAVY."

Even In Cyperspace, It's a Jungle Out There

*W*hat a world we live in. On April 27, 1998, Koko, a gorilla who speaks with sign language, held an on-line question-and-answer session with humans more her peers than her evolutionary superiors. Despite the fact that thousands, if not millions, of displaced workers and homeless families frequently go without food and proper medical care, we are now giving computers to monkeys?

Perhaps most offensive is that America Online gave free AOL time to this simian, yet they make the rest of us pay for it. Call me a cheapskate if you want but I too am a simian. I'll even eat a banana in front of AOL headquarters to prove it, if they want.

Working with the Gorilla Foundation, the profitable on-line service hosted a "chat session" with Koko, allowing humans to pose questions of the primate and wait for a response. Sources say conservatives in Congress are already working on an amendment to the Telecommunications Decency Act requiring Koko or other monkeys to wear clothes when on-line. They may have a point. After all, how many parents would let their kids go into a chatroom with a naked ape?

The official transcript of that historic session is probably available somewhere out in cyberspace. However, in the interests of completeness, I have painstakingly tracked down some of the portions that were excised by AOL censors:

"Koko, what impact -- if any -- do you think the Internet will have on interspecies communication? Will it allow John Q. Public to become a veritable Dr. Doolittle, a man known for his ability to 'talk with the animals'?"

"HUNGRY"

"What are you wearing right now? Do you want to know what I am wearing?"

"WANT BANANA"

"Koko, it is clear from the actions of Iraqi President Saddam Hussein that his intentions are to be as uncooperative as possible, delaying for days -- if not months -- any progress towards a peaceable solution to the tensions in the Middle East. In your opinion, what should the United States' involvement in this tense situation be?"

"GIVE KOKO BANANA -- NOW"

"With the phenomenal success of the highest grossing box-office movie ever, what do you think are the possibilities of a sequel to "Titanic" and who do you believe should be cast in it?"

"SWIMMERS WITH WARM CLOTHING! KOKO rraARGH.."

"Social Security has come under fire by those under 30 who believe they will receive no benefits from the 63-year-old program, and by those over 60 who worry that reform efforts will reduce -- if not eliminate -- the amount they are owed. What sort of reform efforts would you recommend, if any are even possible?"

"KOKO -- HUNGRY -- ANGRY – BREAK KEYBOArsj2%E! [transfer interrupted]"*

"Koko, in some quarters, taxpayers are calling for a 'flat tax' to simplify the U.S. Tax Code and to reduce their own tax burden while simultaneously forcing the federal government to do more with less. Others maintain that a 'flat tax' would be a regressive tax, forcing those with comparatively lower incomes to shoulder a proportionately larger tax burden. Do you believe a 'flat tax' is a step in the right direction or would a more graduated scale, similar to what is currently in place, be a more equitable solution?"

"BANANA -- NOW -- OR KOKO GO CRAZY KILL TOURIST YAAAUG[transfer interrupted]"

Though this portion of the chat session was removed from the official transcript, the facts speak for themselves. Koko, a gorilla with a nearly 1,000 word vocabulary, has more definable and clearly articulated ideas on tax reform, Social Security and contemporary foreign relations than many elected officials. It may only be a matter of time before Koko is booked to appear on either the "MacLaughlin Group," "Meet the Press" or "Politically Incorrect with Bill Maher." What's more, Koko likely will get preferential parking at each show. After all, she is "evolutionarily-challenged" and qualifies for the good parking spaces under the Americans with Disabilities Act.

Time will tell what's next for Koko. Until then, if you find yourself discussing tax reform with someone in an on-line chatroom, bring a banana -- you may be chatting with a hungry naked gorilla. Even in cyberspace, it's a jungle out there.

Is Barbie a Serial (Numbered) Killer?

*W*hat do James Earl Ray, Mark David Chapman and Barbie have in common? Besides the fact that all celebrate their birthdays the second week of March, they are also guilty of murder. One killed Dr. Martin Luther King, Jr., one killed John Lennon, and the other has killed numerous women -- from Karen Carpenter to Jon-Benet Ramsey. But let's begin at the beginning, shall we?

Barbie was "born" on March 9, 1959. Ironically, folks in those days never imagined her womanly figure and painted face would be so popular, nor that her physique would serve to promote a hazardous ideal of the feminine form. Since then, more than half a billion Barbies have been sold. In other words, if every Barbie ever made were laid end to end, they would circle the globe nearly four times.[9] According to Mattel, Inc., Barbie gets about a hundred new outfits each year and, since her creation, over 105 million yards of fabric have been used to create her clothes -- making Mattel America's fourth largest maker of women's clothes.

Not to worry -- Barbie can afford her mammoth wardrobe. Over the years, she has held several jobs. She's been everything from a teacher to a gymnast, including an astronaut, veterinarian, soldier, singer, aerobics instructor, flight attendant and, yes, even a model. Some believe this reflects the diversity of women in the modern workplace, though others feel it shows Barbie can't hold a steady job. Comedians are more familiar with the "Divorce Barbie," which comes with Ken's Corvette and half of his Malibu Dream House.

Over the years, Mattel's Barbie effort suffered problems. Co-creator Ruth Handler, who named Barbie after her own daughter, was indicted in 1974 by a federal grand jury on securities fraud. Some Barbie-related innovations were missteps, from the talking Barbie who pouted "Math class is tough!" to the discovery that

---

[9] There's an old joke about girls from Vassar that starts the same way, but finishes quite differently.

Barbie's Dream House has no wheelchair access ramp for her new disabled friend, Share-A-Smile Becky.

With Barbie being one of the most conspicuous forces in America's textile industry, she clearly is a determining factor in women's fashion. Unfortunately, she hasn't been the best role model. With a vacuous gaze and docile personality, coupled with an impossible body style -- 39-18-33, according to experts -- Barbie has led thousands of women to unnecessary cosmetic surgery, and eating disorders like anorexia and bulimia nervosa. The death of singer Karen Carpenter only underscores the danger inherent in self-image problems engendered by Barbie and the fashion industry in general. Be that as it may, Barbie's sales continue to set records.

> "Until Barbie eats a piece of birthday cake, she will continue to give unfortunate new meaning to the term 'killer body.'"

Few dolls can match Barbie's enduring popularity, which may be due to the many adults who still collect her wardrobes and accessories. The desire among adults to play "dress-up" seems rampant among Barbie's adult collectors. It can be argued that children's beauty pageants, such as those associated with the death of Jon-Benet Ramsey, are gross manifestations of a Barbie-based "Peter Pan" complex. As in the timeless tale of Peter Pan, a boy who retreats into a fantasyland to avoid growing up, Barbie doll fans remain in touch with their inner child by externalizing them in their dolls. Isn't it possible that dressing up one's children for pageants is a manifestation of Barbie-style make-believe?

While Barbie is marketed towards girls, others are moving into the increasingly active "dolls for boys" market. Hasbro hopes its new campaign to commemorate Medal of Honor winners will help to revitalize sales of the forever-embattled G.I. Joe. In late 1998, Hasbro unveiled the first of its "Classic Collection" series -- a limited edition G.I. Joe-version of Mitchell Paige, a Marine who won the Medal of Honor in 1943 for singlehandedly defending a landing strip in Guadalcanal from Japanese troops. Other dolls are entering the male market as well. One is a 12-inch doll of Minnesota Governor Jesse Ventura, which comes with three clothing options: a dark, gubernatorial-looking suit, a Navy SEAL outfit, and casual wear, including a black sweatshirt with the logo of Champlin Park High School where he volunteers as a football coach. This makes Ventura the first American governor to truly have a "kung-fu grip."

Sales of these new dolls will reveal much about the nature of Americans. Perhaps we prefer to live vicariously through little plastic people. This might explain the popularity of Pamela Anderson Lee and the cast of "Baywatch." However, if Barbie wants to be a socially-conscious reflection of modern life, Mattel should work harder to make her measurements more realistic. Until Barbie eats a piece of birthday cake, she will continue to give unfortunate new meaning to the term "killer body."

Kiddie Porn Spelled "C-P-S-C"

*I*f you believe the "Gap for Kids" is essentially a "Frederick's for Pedophiles," you'll surely agree the Consumer Product Safety Commission (CPSC) belongs on the FBI's National Sex Offender Registry. "Why?" you may ask. Simple. The CPSC -- the nation's taxpayer-funded nervous nanny -- is bent on stripping America's children naked and leaving them that way. In the name of safety, of course. In fact, the CPSC has used YOUR tax dollars to put pictures of nude children on its heavily-trafficked website.

Because Americans frequently pursue life, liberty and other dangerous forms of happiness, the CPSC has instructed you to wear helmets when you bike. It also has told you not to stick your fingers in light sockets and to avoid letting long hair dangle around drill presses. Given a chance, the CPSC would probably illegalize running with scissors, swimming less than thirty minutes after eating and voting for third-party candidates.

Doubters need only be made aware of the CPSC's attempt to discourage parents from sleeping with their babies. Citing a study that reported 121 infant deaths over an eight-year period due to "overlaying" -- which occurs when a parent, caregiver or sibling accidentally suffocates a baby while both are sleeping in an adult bed -- the CPSC issued a stern warning on September 29, 1999, against allowing children under 2 years old to sleep in bed with their parents. This, of course, prompted an immediate backlash from breast-feeding advocates, pediatricians who support "co-sleeping" with children, and anthropologists who report that parents sleeping with their babies is considered a social norm in most world cultures. In legal circles, this is called the "Woody Allen" defense, in honor of a noted co-sleeper's protests when confronted by his then-wife Mia Farrow about her daughter Soon-Yi Previn.

Parents across the nation are enraged at the CPSC for telling them what to do in their own homes with their own children. "If sleeping with my children is outlawed," said one angry parent, "only outlaws will sleep with my children." Moreover, the CPSC's boudoir boycott came on the heels of its "suggestion" August 11, 1999, to "[r]emove drawstrings on hoods or around the neck... Since 1985, 22 children have died when drawstrings caught on school buses, playground equipment and other products."

The CPSC has a history of taking kids' clothes off. On June 2, 1997, the commission announced the recall of "more than 86,000 Levi's brand girls' dresses. The dresses' snaps can become detached, presenting a choking hazard to young children." Three months earlier, according to a press release, the CPSC recalled "about 30,000 'Little Miracles' rompers for infant boys." CPSC researchers revealed that the paint on the rompers' cap snaps presented a potential lead poisoning hazard to young children, and concluded the snaps violate the ban on lead paint under the U.S. Consumer Product Safety Act.

Since 1993, the CPSC has recalled nearly 80,000 items of children's clothing, including about 3,000 Little Levi's Koveralls and Shortalls said to feature snap fasteners on the inside legs of the garments which may separate -- creating a potential choking risk to children. In truth, the only kids limber enough to get their little mouths down near those pesky leaden snap fasteners are circus children -- and double-jointed circus kids at that. Thankfully, most circus children are too busy wearing monkey suits on the high-wire to attempt something risky like lodging their head in their pants legs or swallowing poisonous snap fasteners.

In 1994, the CPSC recalled three styles of romper garment sets by Best Wear, Inc., which featured necklaces with a stuffed doll hanging at the end. According to the CPSC's press release, "the stuffed doll necklaces present a potential strangulation hazard when hung around the necks of crib-aged children." That same year, the commission recalled approximately 6,500 boys' newborn 3-piece outfits consisting of a blue and white cotton/polyester cardigan sweater, short sleeved top, and checked pants. The CPSC press release described the possibility of a snap fastener on the cardigans choking infants. A horrific fate for any new parent, granted, but one the child surely would prefer over wearing golf clothes at such an early age.

With a federal agency so bent on disrobing America's children – under the auspices of guarding them against potential choking and poisoning hazards -- the CPSC may be doing more to fan the flames of pedophilia than to ensure the nation's safety. It certainly doesn't help to put pictures of naked children on a government website. If tax dollars are to support pedophilia and other blasphemies, it should be done the old-fashioned way -- through the National Endowment for the Arts.

Be True To Your School (of the Americas)

*I*n an effort to get increasingly violent peaceniks off their backs, members of Congress voted to de-fund, and thereby close, the infamous "School of the Americas" at Ft. Benning, Georgia. For decades, the facility trained rebels and militaries alike to promote democracy and other American interests throughout the world, notably in Cuba and South America, with torture and assassination. However, due to mounting public pressure that the school served to promote the interests of despots -- like Panamanian alumnus Manuel Noriega and AARP -- and that torture and assassination were inherently at odds with traditional American values, the facility was de-funded in 1999. Later, funding was partially restored, though the facility was given a kinder, gentler name—the Defense Institute for Hemispheric Security Concerns."

As a strong believer in education, I've come up with a few options the school may want to think about. Congress could create federal vouchers to help attendees get their training at any university with a bell tower. Say what you want about Charles Whitman's shooting from a bell tower in 1966, but the University of Texas' track team has been tough to beat ever since. Another possibility is to create a "Community College of the Americas," to train terrorists who are afraid or unable to leave their hometowns, or a "Home School of the Americas" so assassins could continue their training in the privacy of their own homes.

Home schooling has taken its share of condemnation. Many are worried that, if home schools replace their public counterparts, athletic competition among kids will be impaired. Not that children aren't naturally competitive anyway but, when the Smith kids of Elm Street play the Smith kids from Pine Street, it can get a little confusing. This is why schools have team mascots. However, with millions of homeschool athletic teams, there is sure to be a shortage of mascots. They can't all be Tigers, Wildcats and Chargers.

Someone I spoke with about this suggested every homeschool team use their family pets as mascots. This seems reasonable, though it will be hard to imagine neighborhoods rallying behind the Smith Cocker Spaniels when they play the Smith Tropical Fish. Unfortunately, this practice would not apply evenly. Not all families have pets, meaning that some homeschool teams might not get a mascot. When I grew up, I didn't have a pet. Instead, our grandmother lived with us. Frankly, she was more like a houseplant than a pet. We took her for walks, sure, and we sometimes would clean her litter box -- but it wasn't the same as having a labrador or a tropical fish. In theory, it would be tough to rally behind a team called the Grannies. Unless they're from the School of the Americas, from which I've digressed.

Perhaps the best option for the School of the Americas is to simply change their target market. With most of South America either fully democratized under the watchful eye of America's vote-counting ex-President Jimmy Carter, the School of the Americas needs to shift its sights, so to speak, to emerging markets -- chiefly, schoolkids.

With public schools littered with gunshot wounds and pre-teen "hall rage," the School of the Americas should capitalize on the wisdom of the adage "A good defense is a strong offense." If we teach kids to be trained assassins, an atmosphere of détente will fall across public schools. What kid is going to shoot at his locker partner if he knows his locker partner may be aiming at him? The Cold War was a success in large part because of this healthy paranoia, and had the added advantage of creating millions of jobs. The School of the Americas can help reinvigorate a sagging military-industrial economy by teaching schoolkids to fend for themselves.

In addition, it would give the National Honor Society a much-needed shot in the arm. By rewarding good grades with high-quality flak jackets, students will benefit from academe's "publish or perish" mentality. Students on the honor roll would get the fancy, armor-piercing-proof flak vests, while more average students would get lower-grade vests. Students who are failing could be given waterproof vests or life preservers. They wouldn't know -- this is why they're failing. There's a lot they don't understand. Moreover, if slower students are shot through their life preservers, it would promote Darwin's notion of evolution through survival of the fittest and be a lesson to the others. Kansas' Board of Education, for example.

Clearly, the School of the Americas has a bright future ahead of it. As with any business, the key to changing revenue streams is to find new markets and new customers. As politicians wend their way through America on the campaign trail this year, they surely will chant -- as they do every year -- that children are our future. The School of the Americas should take note. After all, you can't spell "gun-toting" without "tot."

North Koreans Struggling to Chew the Fat

*S*ome North Koreans are resorting to cannibalism in a desperate bid to survive their nation's ongoing famine, according to a recent report by French aid workers -- much to the delight of South Koreans. "If we were to 'chew the fat' with our countrymen to the north," said an observer, busily enjoying a meal at a McDonald's in Seoul, "we would say to 'Korean up your prate!'" Giggling, he then buried his mouth in his McRib sandwich and dipped a french fry in his ketchup.

Representatives from Doctors Without Borders reported to the Associated Press in last month that a 23-year-old North Korean refugee interviewed in China told of his neighbors eating their daughter. The report also said an 18-year-old North Korean refugee from the Chinese border town of Yanji described her neighbor killing, salting and eating an uncared-for orphan. Sources say the orphan was jerky anyway, making the salt-related death all the more ironic.

Senate Foreign Relations Chairman Jesse Helms (R-N.C.) is said to be delighted, and a spokesman was overheard to say "Our embargo is working! If only it had worked as well with the Russians 15 years ago." Economists are hailing North Korea's campaign of covert cannibalism, and point to the sudden boom in the North Korean condiment industry -- as well as clothiers like "Gap For Cannibals," and "I Can't Believe It's Not Soylent Green!" -- as evidence of an economy on the rebound.

There have been other persistent but unconfirmed reports of cannibalism in famine-stricken North Korea, which has seen severe food shortages from economic mismanagement and natural disasters. Marcel Roux, a French aid worker who spent more than a week interviewing people, said reports of cannibalism could not be proven because North Korea's communist government hides the truth. "They really clean their plates," said a source, "leaving little evidence to support these allegations."

Lunatics Make Strange Bedfellows

"All are lunatics, but he who can analyze his delusion is called a philosopher."

-- Ambrose Bierce, American humorist

Patience is a Virtue -- Mental Patients, That Is

*C*razy people are short on credibility. It is little wonder, though, with a membership featuring former Senate candidate Ruthann Aron (R-Md.), actor Martin Lawrence and comedians Farrah Fawcett and Ross Perot. Though they are a symphony of disorganization, crazy people share a surprisingly simple agenda -- they just want to be heard by their congressional representatives. For this reason, Unbalanced-Americans are in desperate need of professional lobbyists. Of course, it is no simple task to represent a group whose chief export is what many Capitol Hill staffers call "psycho letters."

Some believe it may be impossible to meet the needs of a group whose interests range so widely, from the government's mind-control of the public through telephones to changing the colors of the flag so the colorblind can feel patriotic too. Au contraire! It is the naysayers who are crazy! Surely, it shouldn't be such a big deal to help the misbegotten of the American asylum. Why does a little thing like a straitjacket make it hard to be taken seriously?

Lunatics are every bit as concerned with politics, if not moreso, than their sane counterparts. Though the Federal Election Commission has yet to confirm it, voter turnout in mental hospitals theoretically is higher than the national average -- which should come as no surprise. Outside of Washington, mental hospitals house, per capita, the highest percentage of political figures in the nation. On a recent fact-finding mission to a nearby mental ward, besides the slew of Napoleons, Caesars and flat-tax supporters, I met not one, not two, but THREE Abraham Lincolns. Surprisingly, they all seemed pretty honest.

One of them even asked me to help with his memoirs. Proudly, I told him he could count on my help just as sure as his name is Abe Lincoln. A tear welled up in the corner of his eye, and he likely would have removed his stovepipe hat to return my salute had he not been chained to the wall.

Later, a man claiming to be John Hinckley introduced himself.

Since being locked away for "observation" after his attempt on President Reagan's life in 1981, Hinckley explained that his time has been devoted to various legislative endeavors. His proposals are provocative, including one to eliminate Father's Day -- a holiday he believes discriminates against bastards -- and another to force the National Institutes of Health's (NIH) genetics research labs to start cloning Jodie Foster.

Ultimately, Hinckley feels his efforts will be wasted unless he can arrange for legislative advocacy. He may be right. Those who think that any interest group can get congressional attention without professional help, frankly, should seek professional help.

> "Hinckley's suggested motto, 'Out of mind? Outta sight!' -- while catchy -- may prove counterproductive."

For this reason, some suggest the creation of the National Union of Tattered Sanityholders (NUTS) to see that Congress addresses the concerns of those with a tenuous grip on reality. While sicking the insane on Congress seems as sensible as trying to fight fire with fire, Hinckley's suggested motto, "Out of mind? Outta sight!" -- while catchy -- may prove counterproductive. His plan includes recruiting people with multiple personalities as they, more quickly than others, can boost membership levels.

Cannibals could coordinate the Washington tradition of pressing the flesh at his "meat and greet" receptions, while split personalities -- the ultimate spin doctors -- could simultaneously work out both the pros and cons of important issues. Those who are in contact with alien races and those with anti-gravitational devices in their shopping carts would be invaluable in providing transportation to and from meetings on Capitol Hill, and those who believe they are invisible would be beneficial at muckraking and other behind-the-scenes work.

Understandably, those who fear mind-control by the government won't have to work the phones. The cannibals could surely find some use for them.

Though NUTS seems feasible in theory, critics contend it is a crazy idea. Were Orville and Wilber Wright madmen for trying to fly? Was Benjamin Franklin deranged for flying a kite during a lightning storm? Of course not. The truly demented are those who believe that the goals of the sanity-impaired can be reached without lobbyists. In a political town like Washington, NUTS is sure to succeed. After all, you don't have to be crazy to lobby here but it helps!

Are You Crazy? Insanity Won't Set You Free

*N*ewspaper headlines in early December 1997 should have read "No, Virginia, there's no such thing as a sanity clause." Doctors at St. Elizabeth's Hospital in southeast Washington, D.C., recommended that John Hinckley, Jr., be allowed out of the hospital to celebrate the holidays with his parents and his girlfriend, Leslie DeVeau. After a series of legal hurdles and boisterous opposition, the request was approved little more than a year later.

With all the bad news we hear each day, it is heartwarming to know that Hinckley, a would-be assassin, not only gets to roam the streets again but that he has found a girl nice enough to take home to meet his folks. "Mom, looked what followed me home from the asylum! Can I keep her?"

This begs the question of how a guy like Hinckley even found a girlfriend. Meeting girls is difficult enough, let alone with orderlies and electro-convulsive therapy involved. Dating must be next to impossible in a mental hospital. After all, the only usable pick-up line is "What's a sane girl like you doing in a place like this?" Dinner and a movie consists of security video footage and thorazine, and it is no mean feat to hold hands with your sweetie from inside a straitjacket. Don't ask how I know that. Suffice it to say experts speculate that Ms. DeVeau is simply attracted to Hinckley for his infamy. Many women are attracted to the "bad boy" type, so it seems insanity has its advantages -- "lunatic fringe" benefits, so to speak.

It makes sense that Hinckley would want to be allowed out of the facility. After being incarcerated there since his conviction for the attempted assassination of President Reagan in 1981, who wouldn't want to take a little time off?

No word yet on whether Hinckley brought gifts to his folks to make up for 17 years of lost holiday time. If so, it's a safe bet he did most of his shopping from catalogs. Not only do malls and other shopping centers look down on lunatics roaming through their food courts, the St. Elizabeth's hospital gift shop has only a limited selection of items: sportswear, like the pro-schizoid "I Am The Messiah and all I got was this lousy t-shirt," and shot glasses marked appropriately with lines to indicate whether the drinker is an "Amateur," "Professional" or "Criminally Insane."

> "The St. Elizabeth's hospital gift shop has only a limited selection of items: sportswear, such as the pro-schizoid 'I Am The Messiah and all I got was this lousy t-shirt.'"

Hinckley's caveat-loaded "family trip" was approved, though insiders point out that it wasn't his first. He was released for an hour under close supervision in 1986 but, until 1998, similar requests had been rebuffed. Such was the case in early 1996, when Hinckley requested to go see the opening of Jodie Foster's film, "Nell." Disappointed with the hospital review board's denial, Hinckley waited for it to come out on video. After viewing the film, in which Foster lives in squalor and speaks only gibberish, Hinckley must have asked himself what he saw in her back in 1981.

In spite of opposition from Assistant U.S. Attorneys Richard Chapman and Thomas Zeno, the hospital worked hard to convince the court to approve Hinckley's release. Special provisions were added to allay any fears about protecting the public, including a requirement that Hinckley be under constant staff supervision while off campus.

Now that the "supervised-release" genie has been loosed, it may be impossible to put back in the bottle. Hinckley will try again and again for supervised releases, and he is sure to succeed.

Rather than temporarily release the criminally insane back into society, it might be a better idea to make guest housing available for family members on the hospital grounds. Instead of "conjugal visit" trailers, as used by many penitentiaries and jails, mental hospitals should consider providing "conversational visit" trailers for the filial needs of their residents. This would be, in a manner of speaking, sort of a "mobile home on deranged."

The sojourner policies of mental hospitals should be given the heave-ho -- and, around the holidays, the heave-ho-ho-ho -- especially as they relate to mentally unstable Jodie Foster fans. In the future, Hinckley and others under observation should remember that children are meant to be sane and not heard.

I Probably Hate You

*I*s it wrong that I hate people who ride the elevator up only one floor? These same people also ride the elevator down one floor, so I hate them for that, too. Ministers, rabbis, Popes, Dalai Lamas and other religious types remind me that it is wrong to hate. Okay, maybe "hate" is too strong a term.

With regard to you people who ride the elevator only one floor, I live to see you die. I despise you so much I would push you off the top of former congressional candidate Mickey Kalinay's[10] 50-mile space tower and rejoice as you burned up in the atmosphere before impacting on the sharp rocks below.

How hard is it to take the stairs? Is one flight going to kill you? Amazingly, you people take more stairs at home than you do at work. It must have something to do with all the Twinkies and Old Milwaukee in your upstairs refrigerator.

No, I was right before -- I hate you all.

Other people I hate include Mr. Otis, the guy who invented the elevator in the first place. Though it had its ups and downs, Otis thought Thomas Jefferson's idea of a "dumbwaiter" could be improved if it were available for full-sized adults. Lazy, full-sized adults who, thanks to the civil liberties movement, get 15-minute smoke breaks every 15 minutes.

For inter-floor travel, I am a big believer in the fire pole. Generally speaking, firemen are not out of shape and they don't offend me. You never see a fireman standing in the rain outside his office, huddled under an umbrella and clutching a cigarette. People who do this -- and you know who you are -- are also hate-worthy.

Smokers drive me up the wall. Frankly, I think smokers get too little grief from us non-smokers. If they need nicotine, why don't

---

[10] Mr. Kalinay, from Wyoming, ran for Congress in 1998 on a platform that building a giant space tower would be a splendid way to unite the nation.

they use chewing tobacco? Considerate tobacco junkies use chewing tobacco or "the patch." Between you and me, chewing the patch will never catch on because your tongue gets numb and then you pass out. As the Surgeon General reminds us, tobacco smoke is a health hazard for the smoker, leaving a wake of unintended victims wherever their secondhand smoke wafts.

It should be noted that, in all of recorded medical history, no one has ever died from secondhand *spitting*. I am half-tempted to learn how to chew tobacco just so I can go around spitting nicotine on smokers. We'll see how they like it for a change.

Who else do I hate? The list has to include public bathroom shamemongers. You know who I mean. The folks who make me feel ashamed when I use the handicap stall in the bathroom. Because of them, I actually believe there are big, tough, thuggy-looking guys who go around "enforcing" the Americans with Disabilities Act (ADA) with blackjacks and clubs. Worse, I constantly imagine the improbable scenario in which a disabled-American is prevented from using the handicap stall because I am wrongfully in it. I feel the same shame whenever I surrender to the temptation of parking in a handicap space. They like this. If we don't carry guilt around like a scarlet letter, the ADA enforcers will give us something else to carry around -- like a broken arm or a fat lip.

My handicap-stall discontent is compounded by the toilet seat being slightly higher off the ground than those in non-handicap stalls. Like I need a subconscious reminder that I don't belong there. Regular guys like me are self-conscious as it is in those most spacious of restroom real estates. We don't need any help from the rest of you who look down on use for sitting high atop the handicap toilet-throne. And as for you folks who squint into the mirror while washing your hands to see if I am secretly using the handicap stall, I'm not fond of you either. You know who you are.

Topping the list of people I hate, however, are Perot voters, drunk drivers, politicians who violate the public trust, and folks who owe me money. The Internal Revenue Service comes to mind, as does my college roommate and that guy at Sears who didn't give me the right change. My relatives also owe me a lot of money --

insurance money, mostly. By making me wait their whole lives to collect, they owe me big time. I hope they don't renege and live forever.

> "People who say 'For your F.Y.I.' are also on my list. If you don't understand how abbreviations work, stop using them P.D.Q."

Others who grate on my nerves are those who clip their fingernails in public. Worse still are those who do so in the office, putting coworkers at risk of getting hit in the eye from clipper-shrapnel. People who say "For your F.Y.I." are also on my list. If you don't understand how abbreviations work, stop using them P.D.Q. I also despise people who use crutches longer than they need to. When you're just walking but continue to go through the motions with what appears to be unnecessary medical equipment, you look like a moron and deserve to have your leg broken again.

Racial supremacists of any kind are also hateable which, one might argue, probably makes me a bigot. I hate people who call me that because, as I see it, them calling me a bigot makes THEM bigots too. Equally hateworthy are people who don't signal their turns, and people who hang up on me in mid-sentence just because I dialed the wrong number. I vow to never forgive that suicide hotline operator.

Though I will be condemned as one, I am not a hatemonger. I am not trying to get others to hate. Quite the contrary -- I am a public servant. A patriot, if you will. By confronting human foibles and threatening to push everyone I hate off of a 50-mile space tower, I am actually bringing about positive social change.

Now that I think about it, I hate everyone who didn't vote for Mickey Kalinay. Without his space tower, society will forever be rife with people I hate.

Thong But Not Forgotten

Summertime is one of only four seasons when people live for the weekends. Unfortunately, it is also a season of danger. Children play outside more in the summer where they are exposed to any number of hazards -- not the least of which are adults who wear sandals. The past couple of years have seen a rise in the sandal-wearing population, thanks to El Nino, La Nina, and podiatrists.

Sandals, like guns, are not inherently evil. It's the careless sandal user who ruins it for the rest. All too often, a pair of bunion-laden feet with fallen arches will walk by in sandals giving nightmares to the rest of us. The toes of older people, too, bent and tangled after years of wearing shoes, are equally unsightly. If there are trees with roots straighter than your toes, do us all a favor by wearing clogs or something.

Hopefully, researchers are working to treat "post-traumatic sandals disorder." I, for one, am still having flashbacks from last summer when I was assaulted by hundreds of violations of sandal-wearing etiquette. As my new not-for-profit group, "Sandals Aren't For Everybody" (SAFE), says, "The golden rule is if you have ugly feet, cover them up."

Don't get me wrong. I am a fan of feet -- good-looking feet, that is. Psychologists call this a fetish. Fine. Categorize me however you want, but know that I am not alone. There are many who are equally appalled at those who believe sandals or, worse, thongs are covered by the "No Shoes, No Shirt, No Service" policies of restaurants and airlines. In both cases, sandals and thongs are in close proximity to food and should raise eyebrows among the consumer safety community. Moreover, business owners should realize that seeing gnarled feet tied to a wedge of styrofoam -- or whatever thongs are made of -- cuts profits by reducing the appetite of folks like me. Where is Ralph Nader when you need him? Hopefully, Nader and his fellow consumer advocates are working on a new book entitled "Unsightly At Any Speed." While wearing socks, of course.

> "If it would help, I'd even donate one or two pairs of socks."

Currently, no plans are *afoot* to change any state's definition of the "No Shoes, No Shirt, No Service" policy. Unfortunately, the real problem is not one of definition -- it is one of enforcement. Restaurants, airlines, and other businesses need signs similar to those plywood ones next to carnival rides. "Your Foot Must Be At Least *THIS* Attractive To Wear Sandals In Here." Socks or galoshes should be given to those who don't measure up, along with the thanks of the rest of us patrons. If it would help, I'd even donate one or two pairs of socks.

Congress would do well to address this pressing public safety issue. I live in Washington, D.C., in an apartment building housing more than 20 Members of Congress. If ever there were people who needed to wear shoes, it's them. Clomping around in their flip-flops on my building's sundeck, I've seen these officials as few taxpayers ever will – tanning. I don't want to say they are out of shape but, on a hot day, it sounds like bacon sizzling up there. Pork is as big in some politicians as it is in their spending bills.

The SAFE movement has a long road ahead of it. As a wise man once said, even the longest journey begins with a single step. Unquestionably, SAFE's efforts will be opposed by footwear pro-choicers. However, their reckless support for sandals and thongs will be overcome. Protect yourself from the unsightly visage, and concomitant summertime aroma, of unsightly feet. Writing your elected officials to ask them to support SAFE's efforts may be the only way to rid the world of the sandal-wearing menace.

Fake Identities Make You More Believable

*T*ime passes relentlessly. Like most people, I mark the passage of time with special moments and holiday memories. New Year's Eve, though, never really has the same emotional impact on me that birthdays do. However, I am coming up on the granddaddy of temporal bookmarks that will make all my birthday and New Year's Eve angsts pale in comparison. It is, of course, my ten-year high school reunion. I am not ready.

The high school reunion, or so I am told, is the one where oneupsmanship is the order of the day. Former classmates and locker partners try to impress each other with signs of success and Tales of Exciting Careers. Ever the conformist, I plan on following these rules to the letter and currently am shopping around for a rental Lamborghini. If you can make me a deal, let me know.

The ten-year high school reunion is sort of like Prom, with the theme being "Domesticity" instead of "Dancing in the Clouds." I made a point of watching several old James Bond movies to learn the ins and outs of making fake identities believable. Frankly, I think my cover story is at least as good as any of his. Don't tell my classmates, though, or you'll blow my cover.

I am reluctant to reveal the truth about what I have been doing for the past ten years because, simply, it is not very interesting. I volunteer at an area nursing home. I suppose it's sort of noble that I've befriended a kindly, albeit depressed, lady resident. She suffers from abject depression, and I frequently console her. She recently got a colostomy bag and is depressed because she can't find any shoes to match. Though I was reprimanded for doing so, she seems to be improving since I told her to "wear red pumps and eat a lot of Jell-O." I seem drawn to helping folks in rest homes because my family had to put a relative of mine in one recently. Rest homes are expensive! We couldn't afford it, so we put her in a rest *area* and called it good. We all still feel a little guilty about it so, to show we still care about her, we really lean into our horns whenever we drive by. We console ourselves with the fact that she has a nice view and that she gets a lot of visitors.

I imagine the first night of the reunion will go something like this:

"What's that? My career? Oh, it's going really well! I have been doing market and advertising analysis for a big toy manufacturer who wants to expand its presence in the burgeoning economy of the former Soviet Union! Russia is just itching to buy American items, as you know, so they sent me to Moscow to do a little research. As all American children of the '70s know, a great kid's toy is the ever-popular, ever-malleable 'Stretch Armstrong.'[11] Remember him? He is the little guy whose arms and legs could be stretched out all over the place, and eventually he'd resume his original shape."

For those who are actually paying attention to this prattle, I would add:

"Yep, I figured selling Stretch Armstrongs in Russia would be an instant success. They don't have anything like him over there and he would be a big hit with the toyless Russian consumers. There are kids in Russia who actually grow up thinking dirt is a toy. It came as no surprise that my research confirmed the doll would be a huge moneymaker over there. To maximize sales, however, my research indicated that the name would need to be changed. To make the product seem like less of an import, I concluded the doll's name should be changed to reflect the Russian culture more prominently. For this reason, the company should call it 'Stretch Marx.' A focus group evaluated this name, and the results were staggering. Stretch Marx does not seem to be the popular name among women consumers we had hoped."

---

[11] Though I never had one, my college roommate did and impressed upon me that Stretch is far more than a toy -- he used it to tow my Jeep to a garage one night when my battery died. In my youth, I always wanted a Stretch Armstrong but my parents were unconvinced that I needed one. One year, they got me Silly Putty and told me it was Stretch Embryo.

I hope it sounds believable. My fingers are crossed that my former classmates will believe the Tales of my Exciting Career, because this reunion is *extremely* important to me. I want my former classmates, especially The Girl Who Turned Me Down For The Junior Prom, to see what a big, world-travelling success I am! There is never a bad time for a good story, right? I fear that, down the road, I will remember this as the Year I Failed to Impress My Classmates With Stretch Marx. Time will tell.

Seen One, Seen A Mall

I am a self-confessed peoplewatcher. You know, those people who like to watch other people for fun. No, I'm not a stalker. Those guys are *addicted* to peoplewatching. I'm the Sunday driver of peoplewatching. Leo Tolstoy, it is said, would sit in the city square while writing because the faces of the people inspired him. I'm no Tolstoy but, if my girlfriend drags me to the Mall, I am perfectly content finding a spot somewhere and watching the people wandering by. Sometimes I luck out and see something -- or someone -- worthy of writing about. Unfortunately, this isn't one of those times.

Why are humans so fascinated with the human form? Because we are the only animal who needs a mirror, I think humans are a little self-centered. For years, we thought the Universe revolved around us. My girlfriend STILL does. In fact, many of the world's religions are based on the notion that God made us in His image. With our preoccupation with our appearance and what our role in the Grand Scheme of Things is, humans are clearly the most egocentric group of people I know.

Shopping malls offer the casual peoplewatcher a buffet of humanity, and observations come quickly. For example, why are there so many people wearing construction boots these days? Even in the summertime, there are people wearing construction boots with shorts. I know the unemployment rate is down but it's hard to believe there is THIS much construction going on. And the boots I see being worn are brand-new! I conclude that many construction bootwearers have never done any construction work per se. Instead, they must supervise from that trailer house office one always sees on a construction site.

Another observation is that there are far too many elderly women shopping at Victoria's Secret. Clearly they shop there. They can be seen carrying the store's distinctive paper bags all over the Mall, doubtless filled with things like merrywidows with support hose or negligees by Depends.

145

Uh-oh -- here comes my girlfriend. We better talk about something else for a little while. Like all these places that sell "fruit smoothies." Remember the good old days when a "fruit smoothie" was called an Orange Julius?

Okay... she's gone now.

She had just come from "Everything Under a Dollar" with a new purchase, so I had to feign interest. I asked what her purchase was, whereupon she showed off her purchase of Lee Press-On Nails. Three boxes' worth, to be precise. You see, she's a very nervous person but she's too self-conscious to chew her OWN fingernails. She buys the press-ons as a sort of finger food, I guess. I don't mind it now but, during a recent football season, she was adding them to the Chex Mix. After I coughed up a thumbnail, we agreed to set some ground rules for the snackbowl -- but I digress.

> "I get bored by myself but I can watch people falling on icy sidewalks for hours."

Why do humans enjoy watching each other so much? We clearly prefer watching humans to other creatures. Anyone remember that ridiculous television show, "Dinosaurs?" No humans were visible in the cast, which may explain the show's cancellation. Humans are entertained more easily by other humans than by themselves. For example, I get bored by myself but I can watch people falling on icy sidewalks for hours. That's comedy at its purest -- where you know the pain is temporary and not life-threatening, but also that it hurts a lot. Seeing someone bark their shins on a coffee table or miss a step going up the stairs is the height of hilarity for me.

The next time you happen to miss a step going up an escalator in your brand-new construction boots and hear someone laughing because you dropped your fruit smoothie, it's probably just me.

That's what I do. I am a people watcher.

Bruise Control and Holiday Traveling

Birds may disagree, but the trouble with flying is the limitation one feels. The seats are too small, the seatbelts are unwieldy and the snacks are notoriously skimpy. The in-flight movie, if one is lucky enough to get one, features Charles Grodin and is not funny -- which is redundant. The lady sitting next to you has an oversized travel bag that doesn't fit under the seat in front of her, and the hyperactive child on her lap alternately cries and flicks honey-roasted peanuts at you throughout the flight.

This, to some extent, should give you some idea of why I dread holiday travel. I envy Santa, not just for the legroom in his airborne sleigh but also because he never has flight delays and rarely gets re-routed through Minneapolis.

The only thing worse than flight delays are "missed connections." This is a scam airline pilots have cooked up with the airports. Here's how it works: A flight is scheduled to depart at 8:31am. However, all the clocks in the airport are six minutes slow. Thus, passengers arrive at their respective gates tardy, only to be left unhappy, confused and gape-mouthed. The pilots, meanwhile, are safe in their slowly-retreating cockpits watching the mayhem and making fun of both the unhappy passengers and the harried people at the ticket counter. This is why airports have big windows -- they allow pilots to watch the bedlam at a distance.

For this reason, I have decided there is no more sadistic breed than the commercial pilot. Except, of course, for the airport's Food Court who butters you up by explaining that another flight will be departing shortly and then sticks it to you by charging $14 for a bologna sandwich while you wait. Having found a home in the airport, "bait and switch" tactics are alive and well.

Santa is to be envied for another reason -- he gets the whole seat to himself. He can spread out, pleasantly thumb through his copy of "Who's Naughty and Who's Nice," cross his legs in comfort and otherwise enjoy the ride. Santa has it good. He doesn't have to watch Charles Grodin movies, he doesn't have to move so the lady with the peanut-flicking kid can use the lavatory every ten minutes, and he doesn't get his knees bonked by the Guy In Front Who Leans His Seat Back.

> "I've found that 'accidentally' spilling scalding hot coffee on these people is effective. Scalding hot tea is equally good."

This guy could be any passenger. They all do it. Everyone on my flights seems never to have heard of a recliner -- even though they all have La-Z-Boys in their trailer homes. As a result, they spend the rest of the flight figuring out how to recline their seat (which accounts for my knees getting bonked) and then delighting in their supine splendor. Unhappily, the sounds of lip-smacking and accompanying moans of relaxation frequently invade my knees' personal space. To alleviate such situations, I've found that "accidentally" spilling scalding hot coffee on these people is effective. Scalding hot tea is equally good. The Guy In Front Who Leans His Seat Back will think twice before he bonks my knees again.

Another in-flight curiosity is the preponderance of tiny snacks. A half a can of soda is supposed to last me to Atlanta? And who eats bags of peanuts that size? They are tough to open, and one feels like a fool fishing around in there with one's salt-encrusted index finger fumbling for the next goober to grab.

For some reason, the airline industry seems to think Americans love sitting around in cramped quarters eating peanuts. In fact, the only time Americans eat peanuts is when they are flying and then only because they are free. How many Americans rush out to the grocery store to buy peanuts when they are low? It's a sure bet that *some* folks buy peanuts from grocery stores but only those folks whose job it is to restock the airlines. Americans like peanut butter. Americans love chocolate-covered peanuts and we sometimes will even eat them out of the shell, so long as a sporting event is going on nearby. However, the only place Americans regularly eat honey-roasted peanuts is at 30,000 feet straight up -- probably because the air is thin up there and we aren't thinking clearly. Through the mid-1990s, Congress was reluctant to cut subsidies to peanut farmers in

Georgia. This may be due to the large peanut interests in former House Speaker Newt Gingrich's congressional district and to the large airline interests in Atlanta. It all makes sense.

Next year, my New Year's resolution will be to hitch a ride to my parent's place with Santa. He's headed that way anyway. However, Santa had better not bonk my knees with his reclining seatback because I'll be packing a thermos full of coffee -- just in case.

For Those About To Walk...

*O*ccasionally, I am asked to give speeches to large groups. This year, I gave the commencement address to a graduating class of high school seniors. It is a difficult job, trying to sell young people on what is, in fact, a most dreadful place: The real world. What follows is my address to this year's graduating class:

Across the country this week, millions of young people are throwing their mortar boards into the air after 12 long years of public education. Do not join them. Technically, it is littering. We must all work to beautify America.

After graduation, some of you will enter the military, while others will go to college or join the working world. For those of you with an eye to the future, hot jobs of the 21st century include "talk-show host," "talk-show guest" and "talk-show fight breaker-upper." Another good job in coming years will be "funeral parlor owner." With the graying of America, the aging baby boomer populace will require increased mortuary services. As cemeteries grow more crowded, real estate will also be in demand. Contrary to popular belief, plots don't thicken.

Whatever direction you take in the coming years, you are armed with educations more valuable than that of your parents. Need proof? Who do grown-ups turn to when they want the clock on the VCR to stop blinking? You, or anyone nearby under the age of 18. I believe this is why Woody Allen married his step-daughter, Soon-Yi. Whatever the case, you graduates will need your high school educations because, according to historians, the world is much different than it used to be.

Before your class started kindergarten, kids had never heard of Barney -- except for juvenile delinquents in Mayberry. Instead of their own Internet IPO, kids dreamed of owning a pet rock. A Discman was the guy at the record store, not a chiropractor.

Muhammad Ali could tell you what time it was and people thought McDonald's burgers were made of beef. There was plenty of ozone, the prom was called a "hootenanny" and people thought of Jack Webb when you mentioned "fax machine." For those who don't know, Jack Webb is the real name of Spider-Man.

Remain optimistic about life despite the troubles of the real world. After all, you probably won't receive benefits from the Social Security program supported by your paychecks. Worse, today's world is bereft of role models like Mother Teresa, Frank Sinatra and Senor Wences.

> "Skiing without helmets is out, but biological warfare is in. The most popular form of biochemical warfare continues to be the cigarette."

Skiing without helmets is out, but biological warfare is in. The most popular form of biochemical warfare continues to be the cigarette. Thanks to Congress, nicotine in cigarettes was halved, forcing smokers to pollute the air twice as much to get their fix. Topping it off, with all their volleyball tournaments and coverage of extreme sports, MTV is now a bush-league ESPN. If you really want music videos, you have to download them.

A troubled world, yes, but one can always find a ray of sunshine if you know where to look. Fat-free potato chips exist. The nuclear weapons departments of both India and Pakistan are hiring. We even have devices that turn off lamps and things at the clap of your hands. We're in the dawning of the Age of Aquarius.

If nothing else, you should rejoice for having survived public school at all. Graduates are being released from an education system that has become, in some ways, little more than a shooting gallery. For the first time in years, people are more likely to get shot by students than by postal workers.

Fortunately, in response to recent school shootings, the National Rifle Association has redoubled its efforts to improve firearm safety and awareness. As a result, the NRA's catalog sales are up. Big sellers include bumper stickers that say "Guns Don't Kill People -- Teenagers Kill People" and "If Guns Are Outlawed, Only Schoolchildren Will Have Guns."

Congress has organized a Congressional Shooting-In-Schools Caucus that, reportedly, is drafting a bill to illegalize the shooting of students, faculty, or staff in so-called "Gun-Free Zones" around schools. Not to be outdone, sources say elected officials hope to supplement Congress' ban on imported full-automatic assault rifles with a nationwide ban on fists, hurtful words and other weapons of destruction. Such efforts are designed to help you feel safer.

Clearly, you and your classmates have survived the worst of it. Life will continue to present challenges but, apart from finding happiness or PURPOSE in the world -- and then figuring out how to avoid the income taxes on it -- the tough part is over. If you figure this out, please let the rest of us know. Remember that life is a team effort and you'll do great. Congratulations again on this achievement and welcome to the real world.

Take Two Sit-Coms and Call Me In The Morning

Some call it "the 24-hour bug" and others call it "the flu." Call it whatever you want, a lot of folks lately seem to be coming down with "something." I know this because I am a recent "something" sufferer. In fact, I'm suffering right now.

Sickness is vastly underrated. It gives you time to think, to pity yourself and, above all, to watch a lot of bad daytime television. Daytime television is also underrated. If not for television programs like "The View," "The Rosie O'Donnell Show," and re-runs of "Good Times" and "Sanford and Son," some personal injury lawyers would have no way to advertise. Unemployment among attorneys might be a lot higher if not for daytime television. Sure, daytime traffic might be better with fewer ambulances being chased but, with fewer lawyers, there would be... hmmm. I'll have to give this some thought. Surely there is a downside to fewer lawyers but I can't seem to think of one.

With videotapes and satellite superstations as abundant as they are, it stands to reason that someday soon there will be a "Daytime Television" channel. It would constantly air all the lousiest television programs of the 1970s, like "The Mike Douglas Show," "Welcome Back, Kotter" and anything with Wink Martindale. And no self-respecting bad TV channel would be complete without "Prisoner: Cell Block H," the long-running Australian soap opera about life in a women's prison. The show taught viewers many things, like the need for meaningful prison reform, how to wash uniforms in a prison laundry and how to respect those bigger than you -- especially when their names are Marge.

What little I know about Australia comes from TV commercials for Outback Steakhouse and "Crocodile Dundee" movies. However, judging from the cast of "Prisoner: Cell Block H," my theory is that these women were imprisoned as part of Australia's national campaign to improve tourism. By locking up the Femme Fatales From Down Under, globe-trotting tourists now consider Australians as beautiful a people as the Swedes, only with better tans. It must have worked because, when Australia is mentioned, the world generally thinks of Olivia Newton-John, Elle MacPherson and koala bears -- not the Wentworth Detention Centre for Hardened Women.

> "Armed only with a smile, a bumbling sidekick named Mr. Ferley and a pants leg invariably caught in one of his boots, Sheriff Taylor meted out his own unique brand of justice."

"The Andy Griffith Show" is another program inflicted upon the average daytime viewer. For those who may have escaped the clutches of the television tar pit, the show revolves around a sheriff named Andy Taylor. Why no one, in the forty years this show has aired, ever corrected this typo escapes me. If the Andy Griffith character was replaced with Andy Taylor, the show's title should have changed, too. Another thing -- he was one of America's first unarmed law enforcers. Armed only with a smile, a bumbling sidekick named Mr. Ferley and a pants leg invariably caught in one of his boots, Sheriff Taylor meted out his own unique brand of justice. It goes without saying that, in today's television market, "The Andy Taylor Show" would never be produced. With its lack of violence, car chases and martial artistry, "The Andy Taylor Show" more likely would be about a country-style lawyer who helps the innocent in a folksy, down-home sort of way.

By the time the old black-and-white horror movies come on, viewers like me experience headaches. Headaches are a common side effect of bad daytime television, and usually render the viewer powerless to turn off the television. It was in this helpless, headache-riddled state that I watched a movie entitled "The Mummy's Curse." The title doesn't matter, really -- all mummy movies follow the same plot: A museum is having an exhibition of Ancient Things Found In Egypt, and a villainous thief swipes a mystic amulet. Angry at the theft, and at being on television in a lousy timeslot, the Mummy goes wild and shambles arms-outstretchedly after hapless victims. Evidently, they weren't big on sprinting back in ancient Egypt. Mummies never sprint.

If dead people, at cocktail parties, chat about how they died, it must be embarrassing to admit you were killed by a 2,000-year-old shambler who, caked in dust and rags, merely staggered after you. On the other hand, guys killed by man-eating tigers are probably a hit with the ladies.

In retrospect, the Mummy and I have a lot in common. We anger easily if awakened from a sound sleep, we moan a lot and we don't feel like getting dressed before going out. On second thought, my headache may be part of the Mummy's Curse. If Dr. Jack Kevorkian were here, he could put me out of my misery. By unplugging the television, of course.

The Road to Hell is Paved with Don Martin

B lame my small town roots if you must but cultural things, like art galleries and ballet dancing, don't intrigue me. However, because she asked me, I accompanied a lady friend to a showing of French impressionist art. It was the sort of gallery that had once been a mansion. I constantly felt like a butler named Jeeves was watching disapprovingly from behind a plant.

If nothing else, I am living proof that single men will do anything girls ask – even if it means looking at old paintings by artists who, by all accounts, couldn't see very well. Impressionist paintings all look blurry, leading me to conclude that the painters either were losing their eyesight or their sobriety. Maybe both.

What little I know about art did not come from my formal education. Rather, it came in spite of it. From kindergarten through high school, my classmates and I were taught how to decoupage empty milk cartons, how to make hand-shaped turkeys out of construction paper and even how to sketch with coal. I am sure this last one was simply a ruse to get us used to the stained fingers one gets after being fingerprinted by the law. However noble, the efforts of my small hometown's art education establishment were lost on me. Instead, my formal art training came from comic books, Mad Magazine and Chris Otto.

Chris was a year older than I but, thankfully, they held him back a year in Sunday School class. As a result, we sketched and doodled Don Martin-styled renderings on the backs of our church bulletins each week during the church service. He was always better than I was which prompted me to "practice" between Sundays on my homework.

Try as I might, notebook after notebook, Chris remained the superior Don Martinist. Over the years, of course, several teachers asked me to stop doodling because it was getting hard to find my math homework amid the tiny faces and cartoonish figures littering the page.

Then, one fateful August day, on Mom's annual school-clothes pilgrimage to the Mall, I saw him. Sitting astride a low stool in the middle of the breezeway, some guy was actually SELLING his drawings! He called them "caricatures," which I've since learned is just a fancy name for rapid sketches of people with big heads and rollerskates. That one could make money doodling was an epiphany!

With wild abandon, I threw myself into my artistic studies, buying Mad Magazines and comic books like they were going out of style. My doodle production went through the roof, but Chris remained the superior artist. Each week during church, he would top me with a new way to draw buckteeth, warts with hairs coming out of them, and the timeless classic "Man With His Finger In His Nose." Occasionally, I held my ground with my "Potbellied Superman" or "Santa In His Boxer Shorts," but Chris was clearly my artistic better.

> "I remain convinced the Inquisition was started by Methodist parents angry at their kids for drawing in church."

Over the years, we doodled on enough church bulletins to have opened our own gallery. In retrospect, THAT is the sort of gallery I would support. Showings of shopworn French impressionism pale in comparison to the tiny pencil-on-paper still lifes we churned out week after week. Unfortunately, we threw most of them away, fearing they would get us in trouble. Methodist parents like ours didn't think highly of churchtime artisans. I remain convinced the Inquisition was started by Methodist parents angry at their kids for drawing in church.

Though the Impressionist display was tedious, I learned a valuable lesson. The next time one is coerced into doing something cultural, bring a pencil and a Mad Magazine. You might be able to make a couple of bucks by Don Martinizing people as they walk by.

Originality Isn't Dead - It's Merely Incarcerated

*C*reativity is a tough thing to come by. Some have it in spades, while others -- like me -- have to fake it. This is why I envy mental patients because they never run out of provocative things to talk about. Perhaps this supports scientific evidence, disclosed in 1998 by mental health experts and neurologists, that certain forms of dementia bring about profound increases in creativity. Some believe Vincent Van Gogh had some of his finest work while suffering such dementia, before sinking into despondency and cutting his ear off to impress a girl.

Others contend that Van Gogh's lovelorn ear-shearing project was a sign of insanity. If he had done so today, he'd be called a "performance artist" and likely would get a grant from the National Endowment for the Arts. Sadly, most NEA grant recipients are about as successful at courting the ladies as Van Gogh was. Experts believe it may be related to a fear of intimacy, though it may also be due to the many jars of feces and urine on display in their studios.

Don't get me wrong. Mental illness is tragic, and not something to make light of. However, I find "disturbed" people utterly fascinating. For example, from historical figures to prodigal messiahs to Reform Party presidential candidates, paranoid schizophrenics always seem to have something interesting to say. Rusty Weston -- who made his debut last July in shooting up the nation's Capitol -- is one of the best examples.

Thanks to the transcript of a four-hour interview with Dr. Sally Johnson, his court-appointed psychiatrist, Weston explained that he is a clone made by the Central Intelligence Agency. He went on to say he stormed the Capitol and shot Officers Jacob Chestnut and John Gibson to save the United States from "Black Heva," a disease caused by legions of invading cannibals. Weston referred to this affliction as "the most deadliest disease known to mankind."

On April 22, 1999, the Associated Press reported that Weston told Johnson that "if he did not come to Washington, D.C., [he] would become infected with Black Heva." Weston further explained that he went to the Capitol to gain access to what he called "the ruby satellite," a device he said was kept in a Senate safe. The satellite, which he believed was the key to stopping the cannibals, was described as able to reverse time. Because of the ability to manipulate time, Weston assured the doctors that Chestnut and Gibson are "not permanently deceased." If true, Weston's defense attorneys may offer another plea: Not Permanently Guilty By Reason of Time Travel.

It should be noted that Weston links most everyone into a grand conspiracy -- with the exception of his lawyers who, he maintains, have been representing him for millions of years. It is nearly impossible to imagine what it costs to keep lawyers on retainer for that long. Perhaps he hopes to pay off such bills with the profits from a Black Heva vaccine. More likely, his legal team is kicking itself for ill-advised mottoes like "We only get paid if YOU do" and "You pay nothing until we win."

> "The price for such 'freedom' -- usually a straitjacket or round-the-clock surveillance -- is too steep for all but the most desperate of comedians."

Comedians like me, who experience the dreaded "writer's block" from time to time, envy psychiatrists like Johnson who have opportunities to interact with people like Weston. The raw creativity he embodies, free of conventional opinion or social norms, is alluring to guys like me. Unfortunately, the price for such "freedom" -- usually a straitjacket or 24-hour surveillance -- is too steep for all but the most desperate of comedians.

My point, obtuse though it may be, is that America was founded on originality, creativity and innovation. In our button-down world of pressboard neighborhoods, cookiecutter hairstyles and workplaces lost in a haze of casual Fridays, I take comfort from free thinkers like Weston. Clearly, original thought is not dead -- it's merely incarcerated.

Pith and Vinegar

"Wit is educated insolence."

-- Aristotle, Greek teacher/philosopher

Who's Whoming Who?

*I*f jealousy is a green-eyed monster, what does vanity look like? I'll tell you: a big black book entitled "Who's Who In America." For those who don't know, I hold the singular distinction of being the only comedian in America to be included in "Who's Who Among American High School Students," "Who's Who Among Students In American Universities and Colleges" *and* "Who's Who In the East."

This last one is especially important to me, given that the eastern half of the world is the most difficult one from which to be selected. Thanks to China and other heavily populated Asian countries, the Eastern Hemisphere is pretty competitive.

My vanity is being tested by the shrewd marketing geniuses at "Who's Who" who, evidently, have noticed that I purchase every edition of their books in which I appear. As a creature of habit, it stands to reason that I will continue to do so. They should actually call the books "Who's Got Enough Ego to Pay for Such Awards."

Their awareness of my ego-driven tendencies probably explains my recent notice that I would appear in the next volume of "Who's Who In America," as well as the Millennium Edition of "Who's Who In the World." Evidently, each purchase of a Who's Who book qualifies me for inclusion in the next level of prestige. If this keeps up, I'll be in the "Who's Who In the Milky Way Galaxy" by the time I'm 35.

Who's Who books are as honorific as they come, appealing to the vanity of those considered. Sure, there are worse honors but there are also cheaper ones. The "Who's Who In the East" book cost me nearly $300. In fairness, they sent me a nice plaque to hang in my office so I wouldn't feel ripped off. The "Who's Who In America" and "Who's Who In the World" books are similarly pricey. Costly, yes, but at least there is some semblance of legitimacy to the honor. As I've learned, however, there are several other competing honors that sound much more hokey.

For example, in December 1998, I was notified that I had been selected as one of the "Outstanding People of the 20th Century." According to the letter, "the aim of this work is to celebrate the achievements of the world's leading achievers." Quite a noble goal, and more than a little vague -- but even an egomaniac like me is reluctant to suggest that telling jokes to paying audiences is one of the world's great achievements. After all, the President does the same thing each January 20th, but his audience doesn't have to pay until April 15th. I wonder if his name will be in the book?

Lately, I've started to worry about being included in such honorific books. After all, if we believe author Lewis Burke Frumkes' book, "How to Raise Your IQ by Eating Gifted Children," folks wanting to better themselves may use Who's Who books like a grocery list. Given the resurgence of fads like cannibalism -- as revived in 1991 by America's favorite people person, Jeffrey Dahmer -- it is more important than ever to hide one's intelligence and achievements.

> "There's probably no faster way to get abducted by space aliens than to brag about how great you are."

If alien beings come to Earth, their first order of business will be to corral the cream of the crop for probing. For all we know, the aliens are already here, editing Who's Who books to identify new candidates for their space zoos. On second thought, maybe I'll reconsider the value of appearing in the "Who's Who In the Milky Way Galaxy." There's probably no faster way to get abducted by space aliens than to brag about how great you are. My days may already be numbered.

Just to be on the safe side, keep your eyes peeled for the "Outstanding People of the 21st Century." If I am not listed, you'll know I was the victim of a green-eyed monster -- and it wasn't jealousy.

Protect yourselves from the aliens by being humble and overly suspicious of any publication wishing to honor you for vaguely-defined "accomplishments." Whether they are cannibals or space aliens is beside the point -- they only want your money, which is a humbling thought indeed.

Joe Camel On the Endangered Species List

*A*s far as celebrities go, he was as big as it gets -- yet he hasn't been seen on "The New Hollywood Squares" nor any of the other pastures in which ex-celebrities are left to die. If you've been wondering "Whatever happened to Joe Camel?" -- don't you worry!

After widespread public concern that cigarette manufacturers were bent on enslaving a nation of school-age tobacco junkies, the future of celebrity smokesperson Joe Camel was snuffed out like a bad cigarette. However, the Herbivore of Exhale has reportedly been courted by others in an effort to further his marketing career.

Despite the agreement between state attorneys general and the tobacco industry, which illegalized Joe Camel's promotion of tobacco products, it was unlikely that the Dromedary of Drags would disappear entirely. Under the terms of the agreement, Joe Camel cannot appear in tobacco advertisements or t-shirts. However, he is said to be planning on lending his name to a line of children's lunchboxes, Halloween costumes, sleeping bags, pajamas, and hoof-shaped novelty bedroom slippers called "Camel Toes."

Despite these plans, many speculate that the humpbacked pitchman's career went up in smoke with the infamous tobacco settlement. Others disagree. Personalities like Long Island mechanic Joey Buttafuoco, skater Tonya Harding, presidential legwarmer Monica Lewinsky, and even plumber's helper G. Gordon Liddy have profited from their dubious fame.

Joe Camel can, too. He is an obvious choice to promote items like zoos and circuses, not to mention camel-hair sportcoats, and any of the desert-themed casinos in Las Vegas, like the Dunes, the Sands, or the Mirage. Marketing professionals would be foolish to give up the loyal customer-base Joe Camel helped create over the past two decades.

To meet the non-tobacco needs of Camel fans, a cooperative advertising agreement is said to be in the works allowing the Champion of Chainsmoking to endorse items ranging from ash trays

167

and room deodorizers to oxygen tents, iron-lung machines and even funeral arrangements. Some have even gone so far as to suggest Joe Camel represent the seafood industry because cancer is Latin for "crab."

> "What soft-hearted smoker will quit if it means a needy child somewhere will go without health care?"

The $368 billion tobacco deal that prevents Joe Camel from hocking his wares to juveniles, stipulates that tens of billions of dollars be used to fund a national health insurance program for needy children. On close inspection, this provision was a victory for pro-tobacco forces as it discourages smokers from quitting. What soft-hearted smoker will quit if it means a needy child somewhere will go without health care? As a result of inevitable public service announcements like "Chainsmoke for Children," tobacco use will emerge as a politically correct and socially-conscious activity.

It goes without saying that the tobacco settlement is sufficiently large and precedent-setting enough that both the legal and business communities should expect to see "copy cat" cases down the line. Experts speculate that the next wave of litigation may come from dental groups, like the American Dental Association, filing suit after suit against the sugar industry. After all, dentists argue that the sugar industry has been addicting children to candy cigarettes and bubble-gum cigars for years. "I don't know why [dental groups] are coming down on us," said one sugar executive, who asked to remain anonymous. "We're giving them business! If not for sugar, there would be a lot of homeless dentists, let me tell you."

According to U.S. Beet Sugar Association figures, sales in 1995 of sugar beets to industrial users -- like soft drink and candy manufacturers -- totaled 1.372 million tons, earning the sugar industry more than $685 million. This does not include sugar produced from cane, nor that which is sold for direct public consumption. Such figures make for tempting litigation, and the ADA is unlikely to find a sweeter defendant.

Manufacturers of denture adhesives are now promoting a line of sugar-free products, to protect their customers from getting cavities in their gums. Sugar-free gums notwithstanding, candy companies would do well to consider introducing products like unsweetened, fluoride-enriched or filter-tipped candy cigarettes. Candy nicotine patches may also be a good idea. According to rumor, plans are afoot for the FDA to regulate candy cigarettes as "fructose-delivery devices." Sources say, however, that FDA officials have wanted to regulate sugar for so long it makes their teeth hurt just thinking about it.

For the time being, experts currently are reviewing whether Joe Camel would be allowed to promote smokeless tobacco products. He'd be a natural role model for users of chewing tobacco. After all, he's got that big mouth -- one could fit a lot of chaw in a mouth like that. Maybe he will jump ship and promote Nicorette gum. Whatever the case, Joe Camel's future seems as bright as a freshly-lit menthol cigarette -- which is more than could be said for the Marlboro Man, may he rest in peace.

Dumbo May Cause Liver Cancer

Apparently not satisfied with Joe Camel, anti-vice activists are now hunting for additional cartoon animal heads to mount on their walls -- and Dumbo may be next.

The Journal of the American Medical Association[12] published a study in 1999 suggesting that many mainstream cartoon characters glorify tobacco and alcohol use. The study, by Dr. Adam Goldstein of the University of North Carolina-Chapel Hill School of Medicine, reveals that alcohol and tobacco use is featured in 34 of the 50 G-rated animated films released by major studios since 1937.

According to Goldstein's research, 76 characters smoked for a total duration of more than 45 minutes, and 63 characters drank alcohol for 27 minutes. Cigar and wine consumption were the most common, but cigarettes, pipes, beer, spirits and champagne were consumed as well. The study also mentioned that the characters who drank frequently got drunk, passed out, hiccuped, lost their balance or fell over. Disney fans will recall Dumbo dreaming of pink elephants after not knowing when to "say when" to some champagne. Will Dumbo be the next poster elephant for the Betty Ford Clinic?

Goldstein's assertion that many otherwise-harmless cartoon characters set a bad example for children about smoking and drinking is sound. However, he overlooks the positive messages sent by other vice-heavy characters. For example, when most cartoon animals light up a cigar, it typically explodes in their faces.

How better to underscore the dangers inherent in smoking than with blackened fur and dislodged facial parts? Also, after drinking the mysterious spirits served in jugs marked "XXX," cartoon animals find themselves in difficult situations -- either dressed in drag, married to a hillbilly, or both. "Are kids being led astray because someone is smoking in a Disney film?" asked Kathy Merlock Jackson, a film historian and chairwoman of the

---

[12] Week of March 21, 1999.

communications department at Virginia Wesleyan College. "I'm not sure we can go that far."

Prohibitionist zeal has plagued alcohol users since the 1920s, but anti-smoking efforts have increased dramatically in the past decade. For several years, Rep. Vic Fazio (D-Calif.) gave "Hackademy Awards" to filmmakers for glorifying smoking. In April 1998, according to Roll Call, a Capitol Hill newspaper, Fazio's award went to the makers of "Titanic," for a scene -- in which actress Kate Winslet lights up a cigarette at the dinner table -- that he called "a disaster in the war against teenage tobacco addiction." .

Fazio helped create the Hackademy Awards in 1995 with the American Lung Association chapter in his district. Teenagers there gather each year to review movies for him. One has to wonder, though, if teenagers should be watching movies like "Titanic." In addition to smoking, the film features nudity, bad language and about 1,500 people making ices of themselves.

Regardless of their role models, whether or not kids smoke seems a non-issue. While juries typically have sided with the medical industry that smoking may be the leading cause of lung cancer, experts are hard pressed to name even one child who has ever died from smoking.

> "Experts are hard pressed to name even one child who has ever died from smoking."

According to experts, those who die from smoking are typically 35 years of age or older. Rather than cracking down on youthful tobacco consumers, Dr. Goldstein and other anti-smoking activists might want to focus more on adult smokers if they want to save lives. In fact, celebrities like Arnold Schwarzenegger, David Letterman and Rush Limbaugh have smoked more cigars on camera than Joe Camel ever did.

As noted non-inhaler President Bill Clinton mentioned in a weekly radio address in 1998, "Today, there are as few as 70 working days left before this Congress adjourns. On every one of those days, 1,000 adults will die from smoking." Again, the answer seems painfully clear: in order to save the lives of adult smokers, Congress should adjourn immediately. Doing so will send a more positive message than finding new reasons to hate old cartoons. Drunk on champagne or not, Dumbo would surely agree.

Land of the Free, Home of the Bravada

*F*ew Americans recall "Operation Vittles," history's greatest humanitarian air rescue. The mammoth effort in 1948 saw more than 2.3 million tons of food, fuel and medicine airlifted into West Germany, symbolizing how the United States stood by her newly democratic allies who only three years earlier were regarded as mortal enemies. The effort was successful. Perhaps *TOO* successful. Back then, we thought we'd seen the last of a Germany bent on world domination. And we had -- until now.

Recent events lead many to believe the Germany of old -- the feared, expansionist goosesteppers with the brown shirts and funny mustaches -- is back and growing in strength. Neo-Nazi groups focusing on racial and ethnic purity are frequently in the news. Germany's favorite television show is "Baywatch," a weekly program flush with cosmetically-perfect blondes -- proof that the Reich's dream of a master race continues. Moreover, Germany is marching forth to dominate the world's automotive industry. Rather than looking like bucket-helmeted "soldaten," German stormtroopers of today are disguised as big businessmen armed with "It's Mein Way Or The Rhineland" and other catchy slogans.

Two generations ago, Germany's transportation industry led the world only in boxcar production. However, since then, Germany has diversified its economy and appears intent on conquering all its old enemies. In 1998 -- a half-century after the end of World War II -- BMW and Volkswagen battled it out to buy British automobile manufacturer Rolls-Royce. Only weeks later, Daimler-Benz AG -- who made cars for Hitler and his staff throughout the war -- bought America's red, white and blue Chrysler Corporation. Where is Lee Iacocca when you need him? You can bet he would have looked those Jerries square in the monocle and said "Ich bin not selling!"

To the casual observer, Germany's recent automobile success may seem harmless. "It's just big business," one might say. "This is nothing like the geopolitical upheaval of the late 1940s that shaped the modern world." Au contraire. Germany is trying to rebuild its former empire and is even turning on its old Axis friends.

> "Russian cars are so bad, they come with 'My other car is a Trabant' bumper stickers pre-affixed."

The same month it bought Chrysler, Daimler-Benz began negotiations with Japan's economic strongman, Nissan Motor Company, fueling speculation that Germany will save Italy -- the land of Ferrari, Maserati and Mussolini -- for last, thereby dominating the world's automobile supply and crushing all who oppose. The only thing saving Russia from the German automotive blitzkrieg is the Great Bear's complete inability to produce a reliable automobile. Russian cars are so bad, they come with "My other car is a Trabant" bumper stickers pre-affixed.

Military strategists suggest that fighting a two-front war like this is the same mistake Germany made in the dying days of World War II. Taking on Japan and Italy at the same time could stretch Germany too thin to defend against invasion by an elite unit of Kias, Saturns and Citroens. Maybe some help could come from Sweden, but Volvo has never been big on hand-to-hand combat.

In any event, the likelihood of what amounts to a Fourth Reich of Farvergnugen is troublesome. America's dream of a chicken in every microwave and an electric car in every garage would forever be crushed under the hob-nailed boots of a world goosestepping to the beat of a German drum. A brake drum, certainly, but you get the picture.

The spectre of a worldwide German auto-cracy demands that all Americans make fun of German engineering. Ridicule the shape of the new Volkswagen Bug. Make fun of the East German Trabant. Whatever you decide, do it fast. Time is of the essence. As soon as possible, America should stand up to the German automotive aggressors. If only President Franklin Roosevelt could have done so, America -- the land of the free and the home of the Bravada -- might not currently face the "tread menace" of Germany's automotive industry.

Posthumous Awards Worth Dying For

*G*iven the significance associated with the Year 2000, and the advent of what some believe to be the new millennium, many used the occasion to look back on the most important people and events of the 20th century. In March 1999, Time magazine announced its list of the greatest minds of the 20th century. Not to be outdone, a panel of journalists -- including members of New York University's journalism faculty and 17 outside journalists, like George Will, Mary McGrory and Morley Safer -- announced their top 100 works of 20th century journalism.

After reviewing their decisions, there were few surprises. Almost unanimously, John Hershey's "Hiroshima" series, an eyewitness account of the devastating nuclear blast first published in 1946 in the New Yorker magazine, took top honors. Others in the top ten include Edward R. Murrow's expose of Sen. Joseph McCarthy (R-Wisc.), and the Watergate investigation by Washington Post reporters Bob Woodward and Carl Bernstein which led to the fall of President Richard Nixon.

What may be most noteworthy is that none of *my* works are on this elite list. This comes as a bit of a surprise because, given my hundreds of high-quality essays on the American condition, surely one of this august body of journalists would have read *something* I'd written. My piece on would-be assassin John Hinckley Jr.'s repeated attempts to be allowed to spend the holidays with his parents, in which I concluded that "children are meant to be sane and not heard," is as poignant as it is hysterical.

Another surefire winner was my "Booming Future For Air Bags Predicted," in which I predicted the advent of driver-side inflatable priests, equipped with computerized sound chips to give the pre-recorded last rites in case rescue crews get stuck in traffic. Another, more secular use of sound chip technology might be to record the last will and testaments of crash victims. Mark my words -- the day of driver-side "heir" bags is at hand.

If it is investigative journalism they want, how about my expose

"Senators Turn Blind Eye to Deaf Ears" which blew the lid off a massive government-wide cover-up: the use of U.S. tax dollars to provide closed captioning for "The Jerry Springer Show." As I concluded in the piece, our sympathy should go to the vision-impaired because they can't see the waste to which their tax dollars contribute. Publicly-funded closed captioning for Springer's controversial talk show, for example.

Perhaps the best example of my journalistic skill is "Mother of All Government Subsidies," in which I reviewed Rep. Carolyn Maloney's (D-N.Y.) effort to make breast-feeding a protected activity under federal civil rights laws. Though her "Breast Feeding Protection and Promotion Act" had support from groups like La Leche League and the National Association of Guys Who Favor Seeing Breasts In The Workplace, it had plenty of detractors. According to Steve Dasbach, chairman of the Libertarian Party, "Only Congress could take something as personal and intimate as breast-feeding and milk it for political gain."

> "It takes a village to raise a child, not federally-mandated lactation centers."

Opposition came from many quarters, including those fed up with her bill's inherent discrimination against gay fathers, vegan infants, women who have had mastectomies, all-male burlesque shows, the Young Men's Clubs of America, sweatshops employing pre-pubescent girls and, ironically, nursing homes. First Lady Hillary Clinton was also expected to publicly oppose Maloney's bill. After all, it takes a village to raise a child -- not federally-mandated lactation centers. Surprisingly, some of the bill's most vocal opposition came from Maloney's own staff, most of whom have no desire to see their boss breast-feed -- especially now that her two children are adults.

I take solace in the trite-and-true adage that great minds rarely are appreciated in their own time. If so, perhaps I will receive my just due when the great minds again convene to select the greatest journalism of the 21st century.

Posthumous awards are worth dying for, aren't they?

The 411 On Illiterate Chic

*T*he glamour of "heroin chic," as promoted by the entertainment industry, has been replaced by "illiterate chic." Of course, the victims remain unaware because they can't spell it. This became apparent when, fulfilling one of my New Year's resolutions, I spent last weekend at a local music store counting the typos in the rap section. Either there are a lot of musicians that speak Russian, or they don't know that "Da" isn't the same as "The." Bawston Strangla, Color Me Badd, Pharcyde, Silkk the Shocker, Twista, SupaFriendz, Heltah Skeltah, any group with the word "Dogg" in it and that kid Eminem all need to "lerndaspell." Unfortunately, they aren't alone.

The rap section of any music store is a cornucopia of spelling and grammar problems. From Da Brat to Ganksta Nip and Mystikal, typographical errors are in conspicuous abundance. In the parlance of the genre, "rap be off the hizzook with typizzos." To put it another way, Homey don't spell that.

Don't believe the type -- even GraveDiggaz need SpellCheckaz.

Seated comfortably in the tail section of her 15 minutes of fame, Missy "Misdemeanor" Elliott is enjoying success inversely proportionate to her ability to spell. Missy "Misspeller" Elliott would be more accurate. Of the 15 songs on her new album, "Da Real World," four are misspelled: "Busa Rhyme," "All N My Grill," "Hot Boyz" and "U Can't Resist." Not be outdone is the incorrectly-spelled Humanreck, whose new album "Deadly and Dangerous" is both redundantly titled and loaded with misspelling -- and I'm not talking about that skinny girl on "Beverly Hills, 90210" either. Of Humanreck's 20 songs, nine are grammatical potholes: "No Gunz," "Bad Newz," "Shook up Da World," "Abuse Crewz," "On Fiya," "No Gunz -- Erick Sermon Mix," "Skit -- Da Chase," "We Comin' -- Featuring Battalion and Propane," and "Living Life Like a Gangsta."

Like some typographical error-riddled version of Dueling Banjos, South Central Cartel is not be outdone. These fine young

179

illiterate gentlemen are the hands-down, unquestioned champions of typo-laden music. On their 1994 album, "'N Gatz We Truss," they managed to riddle 10 of their 18 songs with spelling errors: "Drive Bye Homicide," "U Couldn't Deal Wit Dis," "Had To Be Loc'd," "Lil Knucklehead," "It's A S.C.C. Thang," "Stay Out Da Hood," "Rollin' Down Da Block," "Gangsta Team," "Shot Outz," and "Hoo Riding' In Da Central."

Pathetic, yes -- but 10 out of 18, or more than 55 percent, isn't bad, considering their 1991 album, "South Central Madness" had typos in 10 out of 13 -- or nearly 77 percent -- of their songs. To wit: "County Bluz," "Say Goodbye to the Badd Guyz," "Ya Want Sum A Dis," "Neighborhood Jacka," "U Gotta Deal With Dis (Gangsta Luv)," "Ya Getz Clowned," "Hookaz," "Pops Was a Rolla," "Think'n Bout My Brotha," and "Livin' Like Gangstas." Between 1991 and 1994, the S.C.C. reduced spelling errors by more than 21 percent. If that's not a reason for a "shout out," I don't know what is.

If South Central Cartel is any barometer for the changing tides of "illiter-rap," maybe we should all give thanks. Thanks to dictionaries, SpellCheck and private-school vouchers, U kan raise ya handz in the aiya like U just don't caya. C'mon, y'all -- peace. I'm Audi 5000.

Pokemon Is Japanese for "Cockfighting"

I've said it before and I'll say it again: I am little more than a 7th grader with a paycheck. Between you and me, the most mature thing I do is to use my VCR to record Saturday morning cartoons. After all, who gets up that early anymore?

That said, I am troubled by the faltering quality of cartoons on Saturday morning. The old Bugs Bunny cartoons were as witty as it got, and "Bullwinkle and Rocky" continue to be cited by comedians as examples of great comedy writing. I even heard Matt Groening, the creator of "The Simpsons," admit this in a recent television interview. Modern children, unfortunately, aren't exposed to the glories of "Fractured Fairy Tales" or the puns strewn throughout "Aesop and Son" or "Peabody and Sherman." Instead, kids today are force-fed tripe called "Power Rangers," "Tiny Toons" and "Godzilla," a cartoon in which the big lizard still smashes things but he's portrayed as a hero. It's very confusing.

Perhaps the most troubling of modern cartoons is "Pokemon." This imported Japanese anime looks harmless enough, but I may be among the first to call it what it is - animated cockfighting. Contrary to what promoters will tell you, it is not a nonviolent game involving "cute" creatures "nicely battling." For those unfamiliar with Pokemon, which began as a video game, its premise is thus: humans capture cute, free-ranging animals that look like stuffed toys simply to pit them against one another in gladiatorial exhibitions until one of the animals dies. Unlike their Hollywood counterparts, Pokemon's creators make no pretense about the purposelessness of the fighting. According to Nintendo's "Official Pokemon Handbook," the battle is "for sport."

Supporters argue that Pokemon crosses gender boundaries by appealing equally to girls and boys. However, the handbook describes "Jynx," the only Pokemon with obvious, if not exaggerated, female traits: "Jynx wiggles its enchanting hips as it walks... With its 'Lovely Kiss' technique... puts its opponents to sleep." Too bad the National Organization of Women has its hands full supporting President Clinton, or else they might have time to focus on correcting Pokemon's unflattering characterization of women. In truth, Jynx may be a caricature of Alice Rivlin, former Vice Chair of the Federal Reserve Board. If you've ever heard her speak on C-SPAN, you know what I mean. Even without a 'Lovely Kiss' technique, she can put people to sleep faster than a roomful of anesthesiologists.

With the new Saturday morning cartoons just around the corner, America should keep a lookout for Pokemon, and a spin-off called "Digimon." Both glorify needless killing but do so in a kinder, gentler fashion. At a time when so many parents are concerned about the violence on television, it is ironic that no one is seeking to censure the deeply-evil Pokemon. I will, if no one else will. My only request is that network executives replace Pokemon with Bullwinkle and Rocky. It's tough to find anything sinister about a poorly-drawn moose and squirrel living in Frostbite Falls.

Maybe my views are a little too simplistic, and perhaps a little juvenile. What can I say? I'm a 7th grader with a paycheck.

Whine, Women and So Long

I'm at the point where a lot of my old girlfriends are getting married. One, whom I'd dated for a while in college, got married a couple of years ago and invited me to the wedding. She also included a note letting me know where she's registered. Like it isn't bad enough to see her wander down the aisle with some guy that isn't *ME*, but she expects me to pony up a gift too?

Of course, I did get her a gift. The way I figure, if they get a divorce down the road (God forbid), there's a chance she'll date me. If I cheap out on her wedding gift, the odds of dating her in the future become increasingly remote. Guys like me are not optimistic -- we're shrewd. We see the big picture. After all, if she and I *did* start to date someday, there is the possibility that we would get married to each other – in which case the gift I gave her would become mine again. Guys like me are shrewd and patient.

Getting a wedding gift for a former girlfriend is always tough. I thought jewelry might be a bad idea, since she would be getting some from that joker in the tux anyway. One of the problems with wedding gifts is that they all look alike, they all have the same type of wrapping paper, and there are so many that accounting for who gave what becomes a real chore. I didn't want to get lost in the shuffle, so I considered getting her a life-size cutout of myself. That way, she would never forget from whom it was sent. Nor, for that matter, would he. I was sorry to learn that those things are about' $500. I considered Polaroids of myself, naked, pointing to a tattoo of her name in my "bikini" area. Sadly, they didn't turn out because Mom's finger was over the lens.

For this reason, I opted for something I thought my ex-girlfriend could really get some use out of -- a book on how to get her marriage annulled. Unfortunately, try as I might, I couldn't find such a book. With all the guys I know who are mad at their ex-girlfriends for marrying someone else, you'd think *someone* would have written a book like that. For this reason, I began writing it last weekend. I hope to have it finished before another ex-girlfriend gets

married. Forget getting me to the church -- get me to the
PUBLISHER on time.

Revoking the Artistic License of Singers

Shattered bats. Sliders, change-ups, and a pitcher whose nickname keeps alive the memory of Italy's fascist dictator Benito Mussolini. Without question, the 1999 World Series had its share of excitement and intrigue. However, unless things change dramatically, historians will remember it with two words: questionable music.

What happened to the days of steam organs, and songs about peanuts and Cracker Jacks? In the bottom of Game One's fourth inning, Atlanta Braves Chipper Jones' home run -- the first home run of the 1999 World Series – was prefaced by Ozzy Osbourne's "Crazy Train." Not long ago, American kids were taught to fear Ozzy because, according to parents, he ate the hearts of chickens, drank blood on stage and encouraged kids to commit suicide. "Not much of a role model," they'd add. Maybe Ozzy is seen as less threatening now that he looks like Stevie Nicks of Fleetwood Mac.

Further muddying the game was the hack job someone did in singing the national anthem. This is truly a shame. Now that the Pledge of Allegiance has been removed from many public schools, sporting events are the only place some Americans can get a dose of patriotism. Unfortunately, in the interest of "artistic license," far too many singers of the national anthem are butchering it -- as was the case during Game One.

Next to the Superbowl and "WWF Smackdown," the World Series may be the most widely-shared of American experiences. No matter one's race, religion or ethnic background, just about everyone in the nation agrees that baseball is a pretty good thing. Some may get bored by the third inning but, in principle, watching a baseball game is an enjoyable American activity. That the opening game of what some call the "last World Series of the millennium" would be polluted by an expensive singer doing her "interpretation" of the national anthem is bad for a couple of reasons.

First, the singer -- whoever she was -- chose to sing "a

cappella," meaning "with no musical accompaniment." Musicians like her seem to have forgotten that Congress approved not only Francis Scott Key's words for the anthem but also the music to which it is set. To sing the words but to disregard the music is an insult to a traditional American tune which, ironically, was plagiarized from an old English ditty. Allowing artists to recast the musical foundation of the "Star Spangled Banner" makes it difficult, if not impossible, for an audience to sing along. It's an anthem, for

> "Allowing artists to recast… the "Star Spangled Banner" makes it difficult, if not impossible, for an audience to sing along."

crying out loud. The crowd is *SUPPOSED* to sing along. This is why it's a short song -- so folks won't have to remember lots of verses.

Second, Game One's anonymous singer engaged in a form of musical "guessing." To ensure they are neither flat, nor sharp, and to create the illusion of artistic style, many singers try to hit every possible note around the one written in the song. When Whitney Houston does it, it's done well. Unfortunately, the anonymous singer was no Whitney Houston and, therefore, should work hard to learn the music as written rather than to make it up as she goes. Dramatic pauses were inserted willy-nilly so, by the time the bombs were bursting in air, her rhythm was off. Scattershot singing like hers confounds musical purists and, again, makes it tough for an audience to sing along.

Until we can get artists to honor traditional American melodies by singing them correctly, Congress should make "Crazy Train" the national anthem. Sports fans seem to know the words, and other singers are unlikely to "reinvent" the song of a scary guy like Ozzy. Moreover, America hasn't had any electric guitar in the national anthem since Jimi Hendrix. Of course, this means Chipper Jones would have to find a new theme song. Maybe he could use the "Star Spangled Banner." We'll see what happens. After all, next season will be a whole new ball game.

Overeating Not To Be Taken Lightly

By all accounts, fall is America's favorite season. Whether it is due to World Series celebrations, Monday Night Football parties or the human instinct to add an extra layer of flab to guard against chilly winter weather, fall is also the Season of Overeating. It begins with Halloween treats, continues through Thanksgiving's blizzard of gravy and pie, and on into the peppermint-soaked holidays of December, capped off with champagne on New Year's Eve and mimosas, if not aspirin, the next morning. Gluttony, thy name is us.

As far as nations go, ours is billowing ever outward. And why not? We've got no role models to pattern our lives after. Everyone seems to be crowing about how "The Greatest Generation" won World War II and brought us to a level of technological and economic comforts the world has ever known. No wonder -- they had Charles Atlas and Jack LaLane to look up to. The modern generation likely would cite Ally McBeal, Lara Croft and Michael Jordan as its heroes, if it could be torn away from "Cheers" re-runs long enough to be asked.

The problem should be obvious: the modern generation has no role models at the dinner table. Clearly, Ally McBeal hasn't seen a good meal in years, and "Tomb Raider" heroine Lara Croft seems too busy blasting bad guys to eat. As for superathlete Jordan, the only things America sees him eat are Wheaties, Gatorade and McDonalds fast food.

> "I've got no beef against those who suffer obesity."

In the absence of nutritional guideposts, it comes as no surprise that America's children are getting fatter. A study by the Centers for Disease Control, widely reported on March 7, 1997, confirms this. Moreover, every year, there is someone who -- through no fault of their own -- is so grossly overweight that a doorway or wall in their home must be removed to haul them out for delivery to the hospital. The most recent example made national headlines when 1,100-

pound Michael Hebranko, 46, was forklifted out through the picture window of his Brooklyn home clad only in bedsheets. Ironically, only years before, he had been the poster boy for fitness-pixie Richard Simmons' "Deal-A-Meal" program.

I've got no beef against those who suffer obesity. After all, new evidence suggests it is more than simple glandular problems and that it may actually be a disease of some kind. However, it is hard to blame glands or diseases when some Americans can't control their bedtime snacking until a forklift busts through their wall and carts them off to the hospital.

Frankly, Hebranko shouldn't be blamed for weighing half a ton or for needing help to breathe. Quite the contrary -- I blame whoever was helping him. One doesn't get that big without an accomplice. If Hebranko could get up to fix himself a sandwich, he wouldn't have needed the forklift to get into the ambulance. According to the Associated Press, Hebranko's diet included 24 hot dogs for breakfast, pounds of ham and cheese, loaves of bread, and other large entrees. Be it a kindly relative who buys the groceries and boiled his hot dogs, or the restaurants that make deliveries straight to the bedroom, a partner-in-crime always exists. THEY are the people to blame. Why they aren't locked up for "attempted homicide," "negligent indifference" or the other legal synonyms for nearly killing someone, I'll never know.

We don't need to wait until the New Year to pledge to live better and exercise more. Simple walks around the neighborhood or occasionally taking the stairs can be good first steps. When the snow starts to fly, your local gym or Rec Center has plenty of activities to help keep the pounds away. At the very least, watch what you eat this season. If not for the good of your body, do it to keep forklifts from crashing through your wall. Your neighbors will thank you.

The Naked Jape

"In the end, everything is a gag."

-- Charlie Chaplin, American actor

Super Tips On Being A "Super-Hero"

As one gets older, one begins making time for important things... such as the realization of childhood dreams. Some dreamed of playing major league baseball, others dreamed of living on a beach happily ever after. All my life, I dreamed of being a superhero. Fortunately, once I hit 30, I was at the stage of life where I was able to turn my dream into reality.

Of course, I didn't just become a superhero. I did my research, and got special training at the "All-American Concerned Citizen Brigade Training Camp and Dude Ranch." Thank goodness for movies like "City Slickers," which made extreme adventures like cattle drives possible for urban people. Thank goodness also for Duke Texas, the founder of training camp, who got his idea from that movie. As I learned in the hot New Mexico sun, being a superhero is harder than one might think.

For starters, there's the issue of the costume. Typically a Lycra or Spandex number, the uniform of the do-gooder must fit exactly right or else the criminal element won't respect you. White is to be avoided as the dominant color of the costume, as it causes problems for television cameras. What good is a superhero if he can't be featured on the evening news? Dark colors, too, are bad as they may show up through your street clothes when you're in disguise. As far as superhero costumes are concerned, tan or beige are probably the best colors.

At the camp, I was at the head of the class -- partly because I was the only one at the training camp wearing a costume. Everyone else was wearing jeans and cowboy boots, and seemed intent on going out of their way to conceal their super powers. I kept telling this one guy, Slim from Billings, Montana, that it was high time he fessed up.

"Slim," I said, "you need to come out of the closet, metaphorically-speaking, because you are only denying your true nature." He took a swing at me a couple of times, but I surely impressed him with my super-quickness. After a half-mile, he gave up chasing me and appeared winded.

As he headed back to camp, I felt sorry for breaking his spirit like that. I should be more careful about my powers of super-evasion because no one likes a show-off. They kept us away from each other for the rest of the week. I continue to hold out hope that Slim understands that superheroes can't truly be effective unless they come to grips with their obligation to society.

I've spent a good deal of time examining the ins and outs of making it in the superhero biz, and have learned a number of things which may be helpful to others hoping to use their special talents to fight crime. For example, research shows that female reporters won't swoon over you unless you can fly off into the distance. Flying is a big problem, especially for superheroes without the power of flight or who are afraid of heights. Villains and bystanders also have little respect for us superheroes who don't soar through the air.

Pedestrian heroes have a tough time of it. Have you ever tried walking or running to the scene of a crime in uniform? Trust me, there's a lot of staring and, on occasion, laughter. En route to a crime scene, I once heard someone say "If you're late for ballet practice, you forgot your tutu!" Without thinking, I made the rookie mistake of responding hastily:

"No," I replied, "I am NOT late for ballet practice."

This was a mistake, as it revealed one of my weaknesses – repartee. To be fair, this is a pretty common super-weakness but it doesn't change the fact that, in order to be a successful superhero, one needs snappy come-backs. Even super-villains are liable to hurl insults, or otherwise try to "get in your head" -- making it all the more important to be armed with an arsenal of bon mots. And for those of you who aren't superheroes, keep your comments to yourself. One shouldn't make fun of superheroes who run or walk to the scene of a crime. Someday it might be *your* turn to be saved, and we flight-impaired superheroes will remember your hurtful laughter.

Getting there:

As noted above, transportation is at the heart of superherodom. More specifically, getting to the scene of the crime is of paramount importance among the superhero community. For those unable to teleport or to fly, it is important to consider a super-vehicle.

"Having the Batmobile may seem glamorous," said one superhero, speaking on the condition of anonymity, "but when you factor in the costs of parking, insurance, and security measures to guard against carjackers, gloryseekers or vandals, having a super-vehicle can be very costly." He added that, due to the "stop-and-go" style driving central to superheroing, gasoline and brake repair costs add up quickly.

"An invisible jet may seem like a good idea," added another member of the superhero establishment, also under condition of anonymity, "until you forget where it's parked or lock your invisible keys in it. Another drawback is that you can't keep it in the parking lot where you work because it needs a runway. So, everytime there is a crime, I have to come up with some new reason to go to the airport. Then, once I get there, I have to figure out if the jet is gassed up. Invisible gas gauges are a pain – and Hera help you if there is an electrical problem, because the owner's manual is invisible too. If I had to do it over again, I'd get rollerblades or something I could take to work in my gym bag."

The Sidekick:

Another important, but often overlooked, aspect to a superhero's transportation is the sidekick. Having a junior partner not only helps to commit additional resources to the war on crime, but it also qualifies you to drive in "high-occupancy vehicle" (HOV) lanes. Consequently, superheroes without sidekicks have to carpool.

Super Hair Do's and Don'ts:

Flying superheroes have it tough. Anyone who has ever put their head out the window of a vehicle speeding down the highway knows that one's hair can get really messed up. In this respect, us superheroes who run to the scene of the crime have less on-site primping to do. Anyone who thinks Superman is perfectly coiffed each time he lands clearly hasn't done enough research. Of course, messed-up hair happens to non-flying heroes too. Certain masks, cowls or helmets often result in a form of super "hat-head" that complicates getting back into disguise quickly. That said, bald superheroes, or those with crewcuts, are to be envied for the ability to more quickly get back into their civilian disguise.

Putting the "secret" in secret identity:

Changing into costume is also a tricky subject. Reportedly, some superheroes wear their costume under their civilian clothes. However, doing so makes you very hot. Imagine wearing long-underwear under your clothes every day -- even in the summer. Unless you have the ability to stay super-cold all the time, wearing your costume under your clothes is likely to result in "super B.O." Wearing excessive colognes or deodorants is critical to the perspiration-prone superhero, especially in summer.

For the record, it's difficult to tuck your cape into your pants without having your co-workers think you are wearing adult diapers. Similarly, superhero boots are hard to conceal, even with over-sized socks and shoes. One would do well to get a backpack for them. Backpacks are also useful for super-things like masks, utility belts, shields, swords, gloves, bulletproof bracelets, lassos, tiaras and spare invisible jet keys.

The costume is, in fact, the most difficult part of being a superhero. If called into action, a superhero must figure out a way to change out of his or her civilian attire. Some believe in office storerooms, while others prefer unoccupied telephone booths.

Though my survey got only one response, the results speak for themselves: one hundred percent of superheroes favor using a cave filled with bats. Unfortunately, all of these so-called "classic clothes-changing venues" have shortcomings. Bat caves are difficult to find in most cities, and nearly impossible to pack in one's luggage on trips.

Other places are not without difficulty, either. Modern offices are climate-controlled, making it hard to fly to the crime scene via the window in an office storeroom. Also, since the advent of "phone kiosks," finding a telephone booth proves increasingly difficult as well. Another problem with telephone booths is that one can't easily leave one's civilian clothes unattended. Villains and criminals are likely to steal them and discern your secret identity.

Consequently, before heading to a crime, the best place to change into one's costume is a changing room in a mall department store. They give needed privacy and recent Supreme Court rulings protect them from video surveillance by store security. Again, make sure to bring along your street clothes in a backpack or a duffel bag to protect your secret identity from ne'er-do-wells.

Remember the Name:

Another important part of being a superhero is having an appropriately "super" name. Sometimes it helps to use terminology related to your superpowers. Examples include "Lightning Lad," "Spiderwoman," "Iceman," and "Firestorm." Others may prefer using more conceptual terms. Words like "wonder," "super," "ultra," "mega" and "extra" also have proven very successful. Others may include titular references, such as "Doctor," "Captain" or "Master." For some unknown reason, military ranks higher than captain are rarely, if ever, used by the superhero community.

For those without conventional superpowers like flight, heightened strength, invulnerability, invisibility or super-senses, nomenclature is especially important. For example, someone able to lift a car can get away with a relatively bland name like "The LifterBug," but a powerless hero could not. Thus, non-powered heroes must overcompensate for their lack of special abilities by giving themselves fearsome or intimidating names. In keeping with this, I have taken to calling myself "Extraordinary Man" because I am non-powered and, frankly, I'm _really_ ordinary. Please keep this secret to yourself. If my arch foes uncover this information, they could use it against me.

With all this information, you should be fine. If your boss asks you why you're wearing sweaty tan Spandex under your clothes, why your head is shaved or why you are double-parked, take him aside and explain that you're a superhero. Don't tell him which one, of course, because you never know which super-villain is listening. Your boss might be a super-villain himself. You just never know.

As the old saying goes, "Superheroing is great work, if you can find it." The hours are lousy, the pay is pitiful, but the job satisfaction makes it all worthwhile. Moreover, the superhero community is a great group of folks. I haven't had the chance to work with too many yet, but some of my favorite recent partners include "Garbage Man," who seems always to be in uniform no matter how early in the morning.

I envy Garbage Man not only because he has transportation and a secret base of operations that no one seems able to find, but he often travels with a similarly-dressed sidekick -- enabling him to travel in the HOV lane. "Homeless Man" is another one of the really good guys. While he usually operates independently and has no apparent means of transportation, he -- like Garbage Man -- shows his commitment to superheroing by being in costume round-the-clock. Even more special, Homeless Man seems to have no special powers, other than super-smell and the ability to confound his adversaries with super-frequent requests for spare change.

All things considered, my favorite has to be "Weather Stripper," a woman who can alter the weather itself -- but has to take off her clothes to do it. Not long ago, we teamed up to battle the diabolical "UPS Man." As far as villains go, he is as insidious as they get -- he damages peoples' parcels, then disappears for days and weeks at a time. Though his brown uniform is a tad unimaginative, I envy his transportation. I am also impressed by his secret lair, the one that nobody on Earth has ever been able to locate.

Health Insurance:

One of the most overlooked concerns to the modern superhero is insurance. Many health insurance plans will not cover your injuries if incurred in the commission of super-heroics. The only thing more painful than breaking an arm in a failed leap from one roof to another is learning that many insurance companies frown on superhero policyholders. Your best bet is to prepare a believable cover story, like "I fell," "I accidentally hit a door," or "I'm just tired -- I always get dark circles around my eye when I'm tired." Take it from me -- *ALL* of these lines are effective in concealing the dangerous and selfless work of superheroing.

Easy Does It -- Super-Liability:

If they aren't careful, superheroes can quickly find themselves beset with liability concerns. For example, let's say you forget to turn off your super-strength prior to landing a punch on your super-foe, thereby causing him grievous bodily harm, damaging his rocket cycle and maybe causing a building to collapse on him. This happens more than you might think. Unfortunately, an attorney might hold YOU responsible for your foe's health care treatment, the costs of replacing his rocket cycle, any pain and suffering visited upon civilians standing too near the collapsing building, and maybe even the building itself.

For your sake, battle the bad guys in vacant lots or deserts if possible. If not, agree to settle your dispute away from expensive properties, buildings or other things that may be lawsuit-worthy. Ultimately, be careful when you punch a villain because they WILL get even with you -- most likely from a courtroom with help from the "Legion of Realitybenders," more commonly known as lawyers.

Whether you are locked in battle with "The Funkmaster," or simply sweat a lot while leaping from roof to roof, one's costume can quickly smell less-than-super. Though dry cleaning seems an obvious resource, the cost of dry cleaning can mount quickly. Moreover, one risks having one's secret identity exposed by being seen with the claim ticket for a superhero costume.

The careful superhero would do well to have more than one costume, and relies both on Woolite and the gentle cycle of one's own washing machine. If you don't have your own washing machine, consider making the investment. All too many secret identities have been discovered by heroes spotted washing their leotards and capes at the local laundromat.

I should mention that I prefer line-drying my costume. I run the risk of tipping off the neighbors to my secret identity, but dryers can shrink one's costume beyond recognition or create excessive static cling. Static is bad news for the modern superhero. Even the tiniest discharges of static electricity can cause problems -- as I learned the last time I fought "Methane Lord," the self-proclaimed master of swamp gas. It's one thing to bring a villain to justice, but it is quite another when you're waiting for your eyebrows to grow back. And, contrary to what April Fool's Dude says, taping caterpillars to your forehead does *not* hide bald eyebrows like one would hope.

If superheroing is in your future, give it some serious thought. From your costume and code-name, to carrying around an emergency eyebrow pencil in case Methane Lord singes off your facial hair, superheroing is not a decision to take lightly. It is a calling which must be pursued with vigor.

A word of warning: there will be *many* who try to talk you out of the superhero lifestyle, but remember: good always triumphs over evil. Simply place your clenched fists on your hips and proclaim "The world can't have enough superheroes," and their arguments will fly away faster than a speeding bullet.

Pamela Anderson, Charles Darwin and Me

Modern life may be preventing humans from reaching their fullest evolutionary capacity. As most schoolchildren know, Charles Darwin's "survival of the fittest" notion -- which suggests that nature weeds out the weak or incapable of a species -- explains many things. However, while it can hypothesize why giraffes have long necks, "natural selection" theory also may give us insight into the aesthetically bi-polar world of tomorrow.

To assist in clarifying the concept of evolution, I have prepared a short dialogue that can be acted out. The cast includes two students, and one Charles Darwin. If acted out by Bob Newhart, just read the Charles Darwin portions:

Charles Darwin: Whew! I just got back from the islands, and you'll never believe what I saw there! A completely unspoiled island, untouched by the hand of Man.

[Child: Until you got there, that is.]

Charles Darwin: Uh, yes... until I got there, yes. But it was amazing. An island completely surrounded by water for thousands of miles... yet it was inhabited by a wide array of animals, many of which can't swim. Lizards, penguins, squirrels... and on and on. How did they get there? Evolution!

[Child: Evv a what?]

Charles Darwin: My theory, Evolution. I came up with it as we sailed back here on my ship, the S.S. Beagle. As I figure it, those lizards are descendants from giant dinosaurs. Mother Nature "evolved" them over the years to be smaller than us, so we can trap them and make shoes out of them. Mother Nature "evolves" all of God's creatures to fill any empty niches left in His great scheme.

[Child: So Mother Nature is smarter than God?]

Charles Darwin: No, I am not saying Mother Nature is smarter than God. Be careful, or she'll evolve your mouth off. You see, Mother Nature abhors a vacuum. This is why there is so much dirt all over. Housekeeping is not her thing. This is why she evolved humans into our present form. She figured we would invent vacuum cleaners and detergents and get the planet spic and span. Say, have you ever seen a giraffe? Sure you have -- giraffes have long legs, long tongues, long necks and generally spend their days with their heads in the clouds.

[Child: Does evolution explain why giraffes' necks are so long?]

Darwin: Yes, Timmy, evolution DOES explain why giraffes' necks are so long.

[Child: My name is Billy.]

Charles Darwin: Well, whatever your name is -- because their food is up high, giraffes evolved ever-longer necks. You see, short-necked giraffes may have existed once, but they starved to death because all the food was high up. As a result, the only giraffes that survived long enough to reproduce were the ones with long necks. Their babies inherited their long necks from their parents, like you inherited your brown hair from your parents.

[Child: I'm adopted.]

Charles Darwin: Well, then you inherited your brown hair from your adopted parents. You're evolving right now, as a matter of fact. When you were three years old, you weren't tall enough to reach the cupboard or strong enough to open the refrigerator, were you?

[Child: No, I wasn't.]

Charles Darwin: But now you can, right?

[Child: Yes.]

Charles Darwin: Don't you see? This is another example of evolution! Since nature put all the food in cupboards high above the floor, you soon will be snooping around in even the highest of cabinets.

[Child: You mean I will have a long neck?]

Charles Darwin: No, you won't have a long neck. Unless your real parents were giraffes. They weren't, were they?

[**Child2**: Mr. Darwin, I have a question about evolution. If evolution gives giraffes long necks and long legs, why are dogs legs short?]

Charles Darwin: Good question. Did everybody hear that? This young...uh... person.. asked "if evolution gives giraffes long necks and long legs, why are dogs' legs short?" Though it is a complicated process, suffice it to say that dogs inherited short legs because, unlike giraffes, the floor isn't very far from their bodies. If dogs' legs were longer, they would poke through the floor leaving them vulnerable to attack by giraffes.

Such participatory activities will instill in the student a healthy understanding of the evolutionary process. Given Nature's need to improve species to ensure greater longevity, greater resistance to bacterial outbreaks and other environmental threats, it should be obvious that hospitals need to be outlawed. By preventing the deaths of the weak, injured and sick, hospitals are keeping Man forever at odds with Mother Nature. As any self-respecting margarine fan knows, "don't mess with Mother Nature." If not for hospitals, Mankind might have evolved natural protections against broken bones, or even resistance to cancer by now.

> "Back then, everything was ambulatory care -- if you survived the leeches, you ambled home to your cave."

Since the earliest shaman announced that leeches and poultices would remove evil spirits and various bodily humours from wounded warriors, doctors have plied their dubious trade. Of course, back then, everything was ambulatory care -- if you survived the leeches, you ambled home to your cave.

Over time, the medical profession has insidiously wormed its way into modern life. Ironically, modern folks hate going to the doctor's office yet we love watching it on television. Thanks to evolution, there is a multitude of doctor-oriented programming from which to choose. Each week, in the form of television executives,

Mother Nature provides "Chicago Hope," "ER," "Dr. Quinn, Medicine Woman," "M.A.S.H." and "L.A. Doctors," to re-runs of "Emergency," "Marcus Welby, M.D.," "Quincy," and "Diagnosis: Murder." Mother Nature knows that Americans can't get enough of the medical profession. Those who've survived long enough to see medical television shows return season after season can thank their lucky DNA that Charles Darwin came along when he did.

The medical industry has saturated the world of fashion as well. White-colored clothing is making a comeback this year, giving wearers the feeling that they, too, are part of the medical community. Doctors are rarely seen wearing dirty, greasy coveralls -- which may explain why they are out of fashion this season. Again. Similarly, footwear has been affected by the medical community. Thick-soled shoes are very popular this year, with manufacturers like Doc Martens being notable examples. Not long ago, one couldn't buy such thick-soled shoes in pairs. One had to buy them individually from a doctor -- and only then if one of your legs was shorter than the other.

Health care has even worked its way into jewelry. MedicAlert bracelets, used to identify one's special medical conditions in the event one is incapacitated and unable to articulate them, are everywhere. Nicorette, a nicotine-soaked gum, uses advertisements showing good-looking, health-conscious people having fun sailing, or playing volleyball, while chewing their product. The downside is that it encourages young people to take up the dangerous habit of chewing nicotine gum, which may lead to smoking. Surely clinical studies show a correlation between nicotine gum and cigarettes.

It must be said that Mother Nature is probably more displeased with the fashion industry than the medical community. While the medical community simply prevents the weak or sickly from dying off, the fashion industry profits by getting the weak and sickly to reproduce.

Sociologists speculate that the human race is evolving into two sub-species: the "good-looking" (pamelus andersonus) and "those who are not" (trulius uglius). Beautiful people have always tended to flock together. From an early age, when physical attributes are noted and validated by others, beautiful people spend time with others of their ilk. Riding to school together in the cars they got for their 16th birthday parties, the beautiful people frequently discuss the latest song on the radio, or the most recent episode of "One Life to Live." They end up getting football scholarships to good colleges, inevitably receive lucrative job offers and, after marrying other beautiful people, soon beget beautiful children. Whereupon, the process begins anew.

Ugly people (or "aesthetically-challenged," as the forces of political correctness would have us call them) behave similarly. Shunned by the beautiful people, the aesthetically-challenged do one of two things: they adopt an eating disorder in order to become beautiful and join various social clubs, or they retreat into a life of despair and personal torment.

Having no other social recourse, ugly people must intermingle with their ugly counterparts. They weren't beautiful enough for a car on their 16th birthday, so they get to ride together on the schoolbus. They discuss the latest rumors about one or more of the beautiful people, commiserate about their lot in life and discuss their favorite shows of the Friday night lineup. They cut class and end up not going out for football. Scholarships from colleges are scant and, by the time they get jobs, they are repeatedly passed over for promotion by the beautiful people. For years, they harbor grudges and eventually resign after vowing to "mess up that pretty face" of the boss. If they find a spouse -- typically through a "mail-order" firm -- they beget aesthetically-challenged children. Whereupon, the process begins anew.

Biologists like us must speak in general terms, of course. This series of steps is not uniform, and does not apply evenly to everyone. Generally speaking, however, a distinction can be made between the cosmetic "haves" and the "have-nots." Beautiful people beget increasingly beautiful people, ever refining the genetic product into what eventually will be a sub-species of *extremely* good-looking people. The same may be true of the aesthetically-challenged, as they produce, generation after generation, increasingly unattractive children.

Cosmetic surgery and other modern techniques can help one appear to be a beautiful person. Beauty is only skin deep, they say, but ugly goes all the way to the DNA. Those who disagree -- ugly people, typically -- should look at old photos. Photos of humans from a century ago all look neither ugly nor beautiful. However, your descendants, generations from now, will see old photos of you. If your progeny come from good-looking stock, the odds are that they will find you repugnant and unworthy. However, if they are part of the aesthetically-challenged bloodline, they will grunt to their ugly fellow cave dwellers that they can only imagine how nice it must have been to be as average-looking as you.

In order to forestall this genetic divergence, we must work to ensure beautiful people intermingle with those who are not. If they are reading this, actresses Pamela Anderson and Courtney Thorne-Smith or television newswoman Giselle Fernandez need to call me up for a date. As a representative of Aesthetically-Challenged Americans everywhere, let me be the first to say it is the responsibility of all socially-conscious beauties to date us. After all, Charles Darwin's theory of natural selection seems pretty adamant about it.

If you are beautiful, female, and want to help prevent a cataclysmic genetic divergence, call now -- operators are standing by!

AREA 54 (a one-act play)

ACT I

MAN: Hi -- I haven't seen you here before.

WOMAN: *(says nothing, casually looks around, nodding her head in time to the music)*

MAN: Are you here alone?

WOMAN: *(says nothing, casually looks around, nodding her head in time to the music)*

MAN: (getting no response, also looks around to see what she's looking at) Do you want to dance?

WOMAN: *(still no response... continues looking around, calmly)*

MAN: Yeah, uh, I don't want to dance right now either. This song's about over anyway. Good call! Do you live around here?

WOMAN: *(still not paying any attention to him, keeps looking around)*

MAN: Oh, right -- I might be a stalker or something. I was just curious if you had been here before. It's a good club.

WOMAN: *(Still not paying any attention, eyes are focused on one person at the other end of the room... waits, and then proceeds to continue casually reviewing the crowd with her eyes)*

MAN: America is in danger of losing its cultural homogeneity, don't you think?

WOMAN: *(takes a sip from her drink... plays with her napkin for a moment, and then resumes looking around the room)*

MAN: I mean, with an increased value placed by modern society on ethnic heritage, and cultural diversity, America is becoming more a crazyquilt of cultural identity than a melting pot of American pride. This is no more clear than on America's discotheques, night clubs and dance halls. America is being invaded by foreign dances -- not the least of which is the Irish "Riverdance."

WOMAN: *(unimpressed, she again sips from her drink and continues ignoring MAN)*

MAN: Here's what I think -- if Congress wants something to

do, they should create a top-secret government facility in the Nevada desert where, away from prying eyes, popular new dances are designed and tested. Such places currently exist, you know. Area 51, for example. It's where they invented the SR-71 Blackbird, the first supersonic high-altitude reconnaissance plane, and its successor, a plane called the Aurora which can travel at or above Mach 5. Area 51 is the birthplace of the B-1B stealth bomber, and other vehicles like the F-117 stealth fighter and various maritime stealth vehicles as well. Some say it may even be the final resting place of a certain downed alien spacecraft recovered from Roswell, New Mexico, in 1947. These are, of course, only rumors. In fact, that UFO is actually located in Bill Gates' rumpus room. You don't talk much, do you? Are you a mute?

WOMAN: *(a slight smirk, but continues ignoring MAN -- shifts her weight slightly as she crosses her legs and continues to demurely review the crowd with her eyes)*

MAN: Well, I like mutes... They're cute, in a silent sort of way. You know, it was once said that the business of America is business. Those days are gone. In today's increasingly balkanized America, our business should be dance. Until recently, dance innovation had been relatively static. The 16th century reveled in the Minuet while the 15th century dance community, having no other choice, relied on excessive curtseying. Prior to the Renaissance, dancing was little more than moderate calesthenics. However, by the 1920s, the world marveled at dance innovations like the "Charleston" and various "square dance" steps favored at hoe-downs and related country-style jamborees. Swing, or the "jitterbug" -- exceedingly derivative of the Charleston -- appeared to be the peak of world dance innovation. That is, until 1947 when a fallen "weather balloon" in Roswell, New Mexico, changed everything.

Since then, domestic dance production has tripled. Through the 1950s, there seemed to be a new dance technique every week. The world held its breath as the "Frug," the "Shimmy" and, for the swinging crowd, the "Cha-Cha," grew in popularity. With a simple phonograph and an occasional lava lamp, such dances appeared sufficient for the world's needs. However, by the mid-1960s, new dance moves were appearing nearly every day. The "Bunny Hop" appeared, followed by the "Tater Digger" -- made popular on the television show "The Beverly Hillbillies" -- and then disco. Are you old enough to remember disco?

WOMAN: *(stops looking around... then resumes sipping her drink, and looking around at the interesting looking people)*

MAN: Of course you're not. You have the air of youth about you. Well, having the military get involved with dance innovation seems logical. It's a national security issue, right? During the summer of 1982, America was confronted almost *hourly* with a host of new dances -- designed by European splinter groups in defiance of the Warsaw Pact and NATO policy -- such as the "Body Pop," the "Robot," the "Moonwalk," and the "Moonwalking, Body-Popping Robot." In those pre-post-Cold War days, the military was focused on the Great Bear's saber-dance across Afghanistan. I've done my research, so I know what I'm talking about. *(MAN sips from his drink and continues)*

MAN: At the same time, right under their noses, domestic urban terrorism, known as "gang activity" -- was on the rise. Inner city tension was mounting yet death tolls remained consistently low. Subsequent studies revealed that many rival gangs settled their differences by "breakin' for it" on the dance floor. Motion pictures like "Breakin'" and "Breakin' 2: Electric Boogaloo," not to mention "West Side Story" and Michael Jackson's music video "Beat It," served as examples of the peacekeeping power of dance. Given dancing's potential for minimizing global conflict, the military should stockpile legwarmers, not nuclear warheads. With an arms race still in full swing, Pentagon officials desperately should be seeking alternative dispute resolution methods. Thus, the military would need a secret training facility where it could focus on training soldiers to be lean, mean, dancing machines.

With the big-screen success of "Studio 54," a fictionalized film about the rise and fall of a dance empire, and the mythical proportions owned by Area 51, I recommend we call this new facility "Area 54." From there, the Pentagon could conduct its top-secret efforts to train and properly equip America's fighting forces with killer new dance moves. America must remain on the forefront of alternative dispute resolution. Moreover, no matter how much it costs, we must dance on the graves of those [expletive deleted] Russkies.

Frankly, I believe Area 54 already exists. Some of Area 54's recent handiwork may include, the "Macarena," the "Electric Slide" and the "Lambada" (formerly known as the "Forbidden Dance" because of its top-secret designation). This may be why the Soviet Union fell. Not because of economic interests or overbudgeted military projects -- instead, the Soviet threat withered in the face of our litany of popularized American dances. We had a virtual arsenal of killer dance moves, and all they had was that crappy saber-dance.

One may wonder if Area 54 is responsible for "Line Dancing," the popularity of which remains strong and -- like a cockroach -- impossible to kill. Maybe Area 54 had a breach of security or something. If so, cowboy bars across the country are paying for it each time "Achy-Breaky Heart" comes on the jukebox. It remains to be seen if it will be possible to get the line-dancing genie back into its bottle.

However, our biggest challenge lies ahead. American dance innovation has hit a creative wall. Worse, it appears to be retreating into antiquated or outdated dance techniques. "Swing" has returned from the 1940s with a vengeance, and America may founder if it doesn't return to creative progressivism. This is why we need Congress to boost its military spending. Without a bigger budget, America may find itself defenseless against an invading armada of people Walking Like An Egyptian. With Pilobolus already on our shores, the invasion has already begun! How long before America surrenders herself to Michael Flatley, the so-called "Lord of the Dance?"

For the sake of America and her continuing freedom, would you like to dance with me?

WOMAN: *(casually glances over, and is surprised by MAN)* **Que? No hablo Ingles**.

MAN: Never mind. (MAN races to a nearby pay telephone, and calls 911) Operator? Yes, could you connect me with Area 54? Tell them the invasion has begun. They'll know what I mean.

Bob Vila and Home-phobia

*M*y shower is driving me insane. The bathtub faucet has been dripping hot water for nearly a week, getting progressively worse. It now sounds like someone is constantly running a bath, and it is driving me crazy. This may be the Chinese Water Torture I've heard so much about. I tried to stop the dripping, but the cork kept popping out of the faucet. Even taping the faucet shut with duct tape didn't work. Stupid water pressure!

I'm no idiot but home repairs are very complicated. Until I discovered Lime-Away, I thought I had a coral reef forming in my tub. Maybe I overdid it. My tub now has a pothole. On my way in to clean everything, I was stopped by Greenpeace and a team from the EPA. Apparently, since I'd last cleaned it, my bathroom had earned "protected ecosystem" status. I can't be sure but I think I heard a spotted owl in there.

When everybody left to go to a "Fur Is Murder" rally, I sneaked in and -- armed with rubber gloves, wire brushes and antiseptic products -- set about the task of bringing order to chaos.

Cleaning the bathroom is one thing, but repair work is quite another. Pathetically, most of the repairs I do happen accidentally or through the process of discovery. This depresses me because it seems like all grown men are expected to know how to fix things around the house -- and I don't. My father did so, as did his father before him. Maybe it's a genetic thing that clicks on at a certain age. Whatever the case, my home repair genes are sleeping late.

Rather than continue lying to myself that I can do home repair, I ought to be channel surfing looking for Bob Vila commercials, or those for Time-Life home repair books. Pathetic -- yes. However, books like those might be my only chance. Of course, this is a desperate move and has about the same chance for success as the Gilligan's Island castaways had of finding a bottle floating by containing a map and tips on boat repair.

The thinking man would simply close the bathroom door to muffle the hot running water sounds. Thinking myself a thinking man, I tried it. Unfortunately, it makes the bathroom very steamy and creates a warm front. The danger is that, eventually, my bathroom's warm front would escape and collide with my refrigerator's cold front. As any meteorologist will tell you, clashes like these are to be avoided because of the rainstorm such collisions produce. Having a cloudburst in one's apartment is a good way to lose a security deposit.

> "Having a cloudburst in one's apartment is a good way to lose a security deposit."

Don't get me wrong. I've done home repairs in the past. Why, just recently, I unstopped my garbage disposal. After unsuccessfully using a plunger to remove the clogged portion, I resorted to turning the "grinder" (I have no idea what the actual names of the mechanisms are) with an allen wrench and vice grips. Voila! My kitchen is free of an aroma similar to week-old garlic and broccoli. I told visitors I was simultaneously warding off vampires and cancer at the same time.

If I were married, it likely would be different. My married friends all seem to know how to fix things. I believe the longer I remain single, I will be trapped by my own ineptitude around the house. This may be true of all men, now that I think about it. In all of recorded history, no single guy has ever been interested in making repairs for the sake of repairs. This is probably how the "bachelor pad," the native living environment of the single guy, came to be. Traditionally decorated with discarded pizza boxes and those plastic six-pack rings, bachelor pads aren't cleaned -- and things don't get fixed -- until girls are on their way over.

According to historians, America's only bachelor Chief Executive -- President James Buchanan -- didn't fix much either, which may explain why the White House had to be gutted and overhauled during the Eisenhower Administration.

Waitaminnit -- brainstorm! I just *might* be able to close the bathroom door if I also turn on the cold water. This will cool the running water enough to avoid the formation of a bathroom warm front. The last place anybody wants a rain forest is in the restroom. The green shag carpet in there is scary enough without having to worry about moss growing on the sink. Yes, turning on the cold water is the answer. It may not be much of a repair but it ought to do until my Time-Life home repair books arrive.

Bob Vila's got nothing on me.

Supermarket Food For Thought

I need groceries. It's been so long since I last got groceries, I am down to eating The Things From The Back of the Freezer. Tonight's entrée -- a turkey pot pie -- is so old, the expiration date is in Roman numerals. When each bite is a test of whether or not an item is edible, it is time to go to the grocery store.

Grocery shopping, for the single guy, is a semi-monthly hassle that is necessary to preserve our species. Of course, since we can't cook, everything we buy either is something that can be eaten right out of the bag, or features the word "instant" or "microwaveable."

Frankly, if Frigidaire wants to boost profits, it should make a refrigerator for single guys. Instead of the conventional configuration, the vast majority of the refrigerator should be available to store frozen, microwaveable food while the refrigerator portion could be reduced dramatically. We only use it for beer and pizza anyway. Something like a cooler with a freezer on top would be a big hit with single guys everywhere.

I've long given up hope of being one of those men who, armed with a full-sized grocery cart and a pint-sized child, dutifully tools up and down the aisles looking for evaporated milk and nutmeg. Moreover, I avoid the fruits and vegetables section like the plague. Buying food that other people have touched bothers me.

I much prefer items borne in the hygienically-sterile cocoon of mass production. Among the many benefits of mass-produced items is that they ensure a higher degree of consistency. For example, a Snickers bar is the same wherever you go, providing a reassuring constant hard to find anywhere else. On the other hand, pumpkin pie or stuffing at Thanksgiving is consistently inconsistent -- particularly stuffing. Sometimes it is made with bread crumbs, other times it is made with rice. Once, at a church "potluck supper," I endured stuffing made from what I surmised were tiny bits of sponge. This is why they are called "potluck" suppers – it's a gamble whether or not you'll enjoy what you're eating. The need for reliability explains why mass-produced McDonald's cheeseburgers will always be more popular than church potluck stuffing.

Don't get me wrong. I CAN cook. However, friends frequently observe that my kitchen repertoire -- pasta of various shapes, Ragu sauce and chicken patties -- seems a trifle limited. How shortsighted they are! As in Haiku poetry, artistic freedom can be found in limitation. The diversity in my daily pasta and chicken-patty delights is imperceptible to the untrained eye but, to single guys like me, they are as different as "night" and "later that night."

Microwave popcorn is another staple of my diet. What seems intriguing about microwave popcorn is the bag itself. After wrestling open the pesky cellophane wrapper, one often will notice a little message printed on the interior folds of the bag itself: "Remove Cellophane Overwrap." This is offensive to all single guys -- just because we can't cook doesn't mean we're morons.

> "Because we feel very self-conscious at the grocery store, single guys typically go early on Sunday morning when everyone else is at church."

Because we feel very self-conscious at the grocery store, single guys typically go early on Sunday morning when everyone else is at church. After all, there is no greater embarrassment than having to spread one's purchases out on that conveyor belt, so everyone behind you in line can examine your lifestyle. For anyone laboring under the misapprehension that single women see guys with those tiny Mama Celeste microwave pizzas or Cup of Soup For One as "available," allow me to clarify. They don't. Apparently.

Deodorant is also a no-win situation for the single guy at the grocery store. If single women see us with it -- especially anything labeled "Maximum Protection Formula" -- they presumably think we sweat a lot. Conversely, if they see us without it, they think we enjoy body odor. The best bet for single guys who need deodorant is to mail away for it.

Toilet paper is equally tricky. It's hard to win with toilet paper. After all, it's either white or blue and usually adorned with the face of a baby or an anonymous cherub. Who can look manly carrying *that?* On the other hand, carrying an armload of toilet paper with the lumbering "Brawny" guy's face on it would send another wrong message. Girls are rarely interested in guys who need the "Quicker Picker-Upper" in the bathroom. Again, you'll just have to mail away for it… or steal it from work.

Thinking strategically, I always pick up a couple of chew toys at the grocery store "for my dog." Unless they have asthma, most single women like guys with dogs. If someone would invent a rawhide asthma inhaler, single guys wouldn't be the only ones breathing a sigh of relief. Most guys don't actually have dogs but, if a woman actually falls for it and comes back to our place, we believe it's possible to win her sympathy by sobbing "My dog has run away -- whatever will I do?" Pretending your dog has been kidnapped is an equally shrewd move. However, staging a dognapping isn't entirely foolproof -- just ask the Symbionese Liberation Army.

My apologies if I've exposed the seamier side of Sunday morning grocery shopping. Such was not my intent. However, everything I've said is true. The aforementioned are things ALL single guys think about while standing in line at the grocery store. Other than turkey pot pies, that is. Which reminds me… I need to go get some before church lets out.

215

America Should Consider Easter Fool's Day

As far as months go, April is one of the best. Scarcely a week apart, holidaygoers are treated to April Fool's Day, Daylight Savings Times, Pagan New Year and Easter. Admittedly, few celebrate Pagan New Year, or the lesser-known Pagan New Year's Eve. Though April Fool's Day and Easter are great holidays in their own right, celebrating them together offers options unimaginable by our holiday-celebrating forefathers.

Chocolate rabbits are an inexpensive means of celebrating the Easter mood while enjoying a good April Fool's Day prank. Simply find a child with a real-live rabbit -- your local 4-H chapter or pet store should be able to point you towards one -- and replace his/her rabbit with a chocolate one. After explaining to the distraught child that, occasionally, God turns things into chocolate to punish kids who cry, you can celebrate the forgiveness and renewal of the season by eating the sinful rabbit together.

This prank is made all the more April Foolish by occasionally eating some of the Butterfinger BBs or even small Milk Duds you'd foresightedly littered throughout the rabbit's cage. Later, you can admit that God didn't really punish the rabbit but that you, instead, sold it to a cosmetics-testing laboratory. You can then give the child half the take, along with the souvenir "lucky rabbit's foot" keychain from the lab with which to remember "Hoppy." If it still smells like cologne or hairspray, the child surely will feel extra lucky.

As a lad, I learned that Easter is a difficult holiday. My mother, a vegan, refused to let us dye eggs because she doesn't condone the use of animal byproducts. For this reason, each year we'd dye "Easter *EggBeaters*." The hardest part was hardboiling the little cartons they came in, through it wasn't as tough as boiling pantyhose. My nearsighted grandfather discovered this when he accidentally tried to make "Easter L'Eggs." The deodorant crotch panels in a pair of pantyhose absorb more hot water than you might think. From that day on, I vowed to make sure Grandpa gets nothing but crotchless pantyhose on Easter. Each year, he finds it less and less funny. Because he doesn't see the humor in it like he used to, I have to assume he has Alzheimer's Disease.

Another difficulty of the Easter season is the abundance of seasonal candy that springs forth. "Marshmallow Peeps," spongy concoctions shaped like baby chicks or bunnies and spray-painted pink or pastel yellow, continue to haunt me. They still give me flashbacks of those horrible orange "Circus Peanuts."

> "Cadbury crème eggs are even worse. Take it from me -- they don't scramble well."

Cadbury crème eggs are even worse. Take it from me -- they don't scramble well. I tried scrambling them, after a failed attempt to make an Easter omelette from three Cadbury crème eggs, some M&Ms and a Marshmallow Peep. Maybe I used too much heat or too little sunflower oil. The firemen certainly didn't know, that's for sure.

Worse, they didn't arrive in time to save my lucky rabbit's foot. In retrospect, I guess it wasn't such a good idea to have a keychain made from an animal that's been doused in alcohol-laden cologne and hairspray. I felt lucky at the time, but I guess the joke's on me. In the future, it is probably a better idea to get keychains made from the feet of folks who walk on hot coals. Even sprayed with hairspray, they are likely more flame-retardant than your average rabbit's foot.

While they haven't all been perfect, Easter Fool's Days have always been my favorite holidays. The only downside to simultaneously celebrating such holidays is that Daylight Savings Time gives you less time in which to do it. Speaking of which, time's a-wasting. I need to find a kid with a rabbit.

The End

"Don't let it end like this. Tell them I said something."

-- Francisco "Pancho" Villa,
Mexican Revolutionary

Special thanks to the following:

- American Licorice Company for making the manna known as "Red Vines"
- Jolt Cola, for obvious reasons
- Chuck Bowlus and Dave Perry of the *Rawlins Daily Times* for taking a chance on me
- Wyoming's congressional delegation and their staffs who let me play softball with them each summer
- John "Otto-man" Ottinger, whose many beer purchases require that I put his drawings in my next book
- John Xereas and the whole D.C. Improv crew who think I'm cool (or pretend to, anyway) even when the audience groans
- Greg Lausch for constantly reminding me that I need sideburns
- Frank King for telling me I should do comedy professionally
- Pati Smith for all her support
- Gregg Boughton for contantly reminding me that the only thing important in life is "Grimy the Sheriff"
- Tim Hart, for his confidence and the title of this book
- Whoever is writing the sequel to "Judge Dredd," the greatest movie of all time
- President Bill Clinton and the Democratic Party, for keeping the political humor industry alive
- Every girl who ever broke my heart, contributing to my general cynicism and subsequent use of humor as a psychological defense … and especially to everybody who bought several copies of this book to distribute as gifts.

About the Author

Doug Hecox developed his unique style of humor growing up in the wilds of Wyoming. After earning a Journalism degree from the University of Wyoming, Doug spent several years working in government before focusing on stand-up comedy. He later earned a Master of Public Administration degree from the University of Southern California. Doug continues to write a well-received humor column for various newspapers around the country, when he's not entertaining audiences in comedy clubs and colleges.

For more information on his latest adventures, please visit Doug's website at http://www.dougfun.com